Working with Young Men

Second Edition

Activities for Exploring Personal, Social and Emotional Issues

Vanessa Rogers

Jessica Kingsley Publishers
London and Philadelphia

First published in 2003 by the National Youth Agency

Second edition published in 2010
by Jessica Kingsley Publishers
116 Pentonville Road
London N1 9JB, UK
and
400 Market Street, Suite 400
Philadelphia, PA 19106, USA

www.jkp.com

Copyright © Vanessa Rogers 2003, 2010

Library of Congress Cataloging in Publication Data
A CIP catalog record for this book is available from the Library of Congress

British Library Cataloguing in Publication Data
A CIP catalogue record for this book is available from the British Library

ISBN 978 1 84905 101 9

Printed and bound in Great Britain by
MPG Books Limited

Contents

Acknowledgements

I would like to thank Hertfordshire Connexions Service, Richard Boxer (HCC Drug Education Consultant), Tony Hunt (HCC Learning Services), Gareth Wynne (HCC Children, Schools and Families Youth Team Manager – West), Ann McKay (HCC Sports Development Officer), Zoey Caldwell (Youth Offending Team, South Herts), Lorraine Clark and Ingrid Davies (Young Citizens Project, North), Khalid Khan and Sharon Lynch (Young Citizens Project, East), Charlotte Rogers (Simon Balle School), Joshua and Sophie Oakes-Rogers (Mill Mead Community School), Jeanette Williams (HCC Children, Schools and Families), Anie Twigg (Hertfordshire Careers Service Ltd), Deborah Morgan and Kevin Stewart (HCC Youth Offending Team, North Herts), Gillian Porter (QE11), Mary Westgate (HCC Youth Service), Deborah Mulroney (HCC School Improvement and Development Service), Jani Noakes (HCC Education Welfare Officer), Mike Smith (HCC Community Team Manager), Zoe Williams and Claire Heskins (Essex Integrated Youth Support Service) whose suggestions for activities are included in this book.

Thanks also to any other youth workers or personal advisers not specifically named who have contributed ideas or been a part of the projects mentioned.

About the Author

Vanessa Rogers is a qualified teacher and youth worker with a master's degree in Community Education. She has over ten years' experience within the Hertfordshire Youth Service both at practitioner and management levels. Prior to achieving national recognition for her work Vanessa managed a wide range of services for young people including a large youth centre and targeted detached projects for Hertfordshire County Council. She devises and delivers professional development training programmes and writes for *Youth Work Now*. In addition she has been commissioned to devise training packs for a wide range of organisations, including the BBC.

This book is one of 19 resources written by Vanessa to support the development of creative youth work and social education.

Her website www.vanessarogers.co.uk gives detailed information about further titles, training and consultancy visits.

Introduction

Concerns that some young men are under-achieving academically, are not developing appropriate social skills and are still over-represented in the criminal justice system mean that workers are constantly trying to find effective ways to work with hard-to-reach or vulnerable young men as well as support those in more generic settings.

This book is a diverse collection of positive activities specifically devised to motivate and engage young men, aged 13–19, in a group or one-to-one setting. Task focused, using a wide range of facilitation methods, the ideas offer opportunities to build self-esteem and develop leadership and communication skills as well as enjoy new experiences. Issues explored include understanding anger, stress management, risk-taking and peer pressure, as well as work around positive relationships and emotional health and well-being.

Not confined to the youth club, this resource can be used in a wide range of settings including schools, pupil referral units, Youth Offending Teams and voluntary youth groups. The activities are appropriate for all young men, and include suggestions for those who have special educational needs or who find it difficult to be in a group situation.

The book is divided into eight chapters that can be offered as stand-alone sessions or combined in different ways to make up a longer youth work curriculum.

Getting started

These ideas provide the young men with an opportunity to get to know each other and become more relaxed about taking part in the activities you have planned. Included are techniques for dividing the larger group into smaller ones, which serve two purposes. They are fun and get the young men moving about, but more importantly they randomly select who works with whom. This helps prevent

11

friends sticking together and not developing any new relationships, or small cliques forming that exclude others within the group.

In this way the young men should have the opportunity to celebrate the diversity within the group and have a chance to work with everyone.

Developing communication skills

This chapter offers activities that specifically look to develop young men's communication skills, including active listening, increasing confidence in public speaking and promoting positive thinking.

Through role-play, self-assessment and group tasks there are also the opportunities to develop leadership skills and discover the benefits of teamwork.

Expressing emotions

Key to emotional health and well-being is the ability to express feelings and make sense of emotions, both positive and negative. The session plans in this chapter create opportunities for young men to explore their feelings, make sense of them and find positive ways of expressing them.

In particular, it provides opportunities to explore passive, assertive and aggressive behaviour and consider how to manage feelings of anger positively.

Exploring values and attitudes

Equality of opportunity and valuing diversity should run as an underlying thread throughout all your group work sessions and practice. However, this section looks at specific issues, including stereotypes and notions of masculinity, encouraging young men to consider their own values and attitudes, as well as those of others.

Taking risks

Risk-taking and exploring boundaries is an important part of adolescent development. These resources enable young men to explore potential risks and consider ways to manage them safely by building on protective factors and making healthy life choices.

It is important to review agreements made about confidentiality within the group before encouraging the young men to share information. Additionally, you may want to reinforce any child protection requirements and remind the young men so that they are clear.

Working together

This selection of tasks and games are intended to break up the serious discussion and facilitator-led activities and provide the opportunity for the young men to let off steam and have some fun. We have found the use of 'positive play' particularly useful with younger groups who have shorter concentration spans. All of the games promote team-building and working together.

Endings

The activities suggested in this final chapter aim to close group sessions on a positive note. They offer feedback for workers to consider the success of the programme, and offer chances for the young men to reflect on what they have just participated in. They can also be used as evidence if you are planning to accredit work completed using an accreditation scheme, for example the Duke of Edinburgh's Award.

Chapter 1

Setting Up a Young Men's Group

Who should come?

Before you start recruiting consider what you are setting the group up for. Is it a request from young men using existing provision who want space away from the rest of the club? Or a need identified by a partner agency in response to a perceived problem or issue? For example, it might be for young men who are at risk of exclusion from school or who have difficulties managing their anger. The answer to this will determine your target group. If the group is to be a closed project with a referral process you will need to spend time talking through expectations and agreeing responsibilities with the referring agencies as well as the young men.

If it is to be a drop in or open-door policy, you will need to think about how you are going to promote the group to make sure that young men know it is taking place. This is particularly important if you are planning to target vunerable or 'at risk' young men. This may involve outreach work in advance of the group starting.

How many?

For group work that aims to look at personal issues, such as stress management or sexual health, a small group of between six and eight young men is appropriate. You will also need to consider the age, maturity and levels of existing knowledge within the group. For example, young men who are already known to the local police will have different needs to those who have no offending behaviour issues at all.

For groups with a wider membership larger numbers are fine, although anything more than 20 will need careful management and appropriate staffing levels. You can always split into smaller working groups for issue-based sessions and come together for team-building activities and games.

What will the young men get out of it?

There are plenty of accreditation schemes for informal education in youth work settings (see www.nya.org.uk for more details), so check out which schemes are already licensed to your organisation. These could include the Assessment and Qualifications Alliance (AQA), Youth Achievement Awards and the Duke of Edinburgh Award Scheme. Most local authorities have a nominated person for accreditation and they could offer you support.

Develop creative ways to capture Recorded Outcomes, for example using photos, video or social networking, as well as the more traditional paper-based methods. It is important that the young men can see what they have learnt or achieved as a result of your intervention in a way that is meaningful to them.

How will you measure success?

Clear aims and objectives make the evaluation part of any project a whole lot easier! Methods of measuring and evaluating the outcomes of work should be put in place and agreed before any work starts during the planning stages. This should include qualitative methods such as focus groups or anecdotal feedback as well as quantitative methods of recording numbers attending and formal evaluation forms.

Whatever you choose it is important to include the young men in the process so that accreditation, evaluation and reflecting on learning becomes a part of the session and not something that is simply 'done to' them.

Boundaries

Make sure that you are straight with the young men from the first session about where your confidentiality ends. Ensure that both you and they are aware of the boundaries set for the group and also your legal duty regarding child protection issues. That way they know that you may have a duty to act upon the information they give and have a choice of how much they wish to share.

Ground rules

The young men should be encouraged to respect differences within the group, such as sexuality, disability or ethnicity. The group needs to accept that each of them will bring their own experiences of school, offending behaviour, friendship and sexual relationships and that no single viewpoint is necessarily right or wrong. The group should be encouraged to consider issues from a community perspective as well as a personal one.

The young men can then consider these ideas and work together to produce a 'contract' or set of ground rules that they are happy to work with. This can be flexible and changed to respond to need, providing all members of the group agree these changes, but should include things like:

- Racist, sexist or any other discriminatory behaviour is not tolerated either to you or by you.

- Everyone should be willing to listen to each other.

- Everyone should be willing to participate in group activities.

Finally, you will need to agree with your co-worker what sanctions will be used if the young men 'break' the contract or behave in an unacceptable way. The young men can then be informed and the decisions incorporated into the group contract. Depending on the age and referral agreements you may need to inform parents or teachers, etc. if this includes being sent home or temporary exclusion.

Chapter 2

Getting Started

2.1 Hands

Aim

This is a very simple icebreaker that encourages young men to share the things that are important to them with new group members. If you know that you have young men in the group who are not happy with writing tasks set a ground rule that apart from their names and where they are from everything else should be done in picture form.

You will need

- large sheets of paper
- marker pens.

How to do it

When the young men arrive hand out pieces of paper and pens. Ask them to draw around both hands carefully. Then ask them to write their name on the left hand and where they are from on the right.

Next, ask them to draw juggling balls in the air between the two hands. In each ball ask the young men to write or draw something that represents them. This could be something they really like, such as art or sport or something that they feel strongly about such as being a vegetarian.

Once all the young men have finished the task ask them to share what they have written with the young person sitting next to them on either side. If you think that they will be comfortable open this bit out so that information is shared within the whole group.

2.2 Hieroglyphics icebreaker

Aim

Graffiti, the term used for drawings, symbols or writing on property, is often thought of as a modern phenomenon. In fact it has existed since ancient times, with examples dating back to the Roman Empire. This warm-up introduces the idea that 'tags', the symbols used by individual graffiti artists in place of a signature, are not a new thing! Using Ancient Egyptian hieroglyphics, each group member will produce a version of their name.

You will need

- heavy sheets of white A4 paper (approx 8½ × 11")
- assorted colour wax crayons
- black ink
- paint brushes
- water pots
- cards with the alphabet in Egyptian hieroglyphics on them.

How to do it

This 'wax resist' activity is based on Egyptian hieroglyphics. You should be able to find copyright-free images of Egyptian hieroglyphics on the internet. Print them off and stick them onto individual cards so you can reuse the activity with different groups.

Open the activity with a short discussion that considers whether graffiti is art or criminal damage. Invite the young men to share their opinions and then ask them when they think people first started to use graffiti as a way of expressing opinions, beliefs and ideas.

Move on to suggest that in fact people have used symbols and letters to communicate with each other for centuries. Ask them to suggest symbols that are used widely now, for example the peace sign or emoticons. Show them the hieroglyphic cards and explain that these were used in Ancient Egypt to communicate. Hieroglyphics work like a picture puzzle, with a basic hieroglyph alphabet to spell out names.

Invite the young men to draw hieroglyphs onto paper, using the wax crayons, to make up their name. The crayon needs to be applied thickly to produce dense areas of colour. As this activity works on the basic premise that oil-based products and water do not mix be careful not to use crayons that are water-soluble.

Next, when the hieroglyphics are complete give out black ink and brushes. The ink should be thickly painted over the coloured wax, making sure brushstrokes go in one direction and that no white paper is left showing through. As the ink settles into the paper it will 'resist' the wax areas leaving the design contrasting brightly out of the wax.

2.3 Pop art portrait

Aim

The aim of this activity is to create pop art self-portraits, using a basic printing process.

You will need

- tracing paper
- sticky tape
- pencils
- paint
- rollers
- palettes
- press print polystyrene tiles
- white A4 paper
- a photo of each participant.

How to do it

Ask everyone to bring in a photo; ideally this should be a clear portrait rather than part of a group shot. If the young men only have small pictures enlarge them on a copier so that the image is clear.

Taking one of the photos, demonstrate how to place a sheet of tracing paper over the picture and attach this, using the sticky tape to make a hinge. With a soft pencil trace the photo leaving out detail to create a strong graphic image.

Now ask the young men to do the same with their photos and wait for everyone to get to this point.

Next, instruct the young men to put the paper picture aside and demonstrate how to attach the tracing paper image to the polystyrene tile, using the sticky tape hinge again. Take the harder pencil and transfer the image from the tracing paper to the polystyrene by using the pencil to trace the design, making an imprint through onto the polystyrene. Point out that it is really important that the pencil isn't pushed through the tile otherwise it is likely to snap later when paint is used.

Take the tracing paper gently off the tile and look at the imprint. If the design is not complete, place back down and draw over again. Remove the tracing paper and paint an arrow on the back of the polystyrene block to show which way up the tile should be when printing.

Once again, wait whilst the young men follow your directions and get their print tiles ready.

As they finish, ask each person to choose three paint colours that they think represent their personalities. Explain that, starting with the lightest colour, they should mix the paint in a flat palette and then use the roller to gently coat the printing tile with paint. After placing it firmly face down onto paper, show how to mark the corners of the block with a pencil so that the tile can be put down in the same place as colours are added. Roll across the back of the block with a clean roller.

Do three or four of these either in a row or to form a square on the paper, each time lifting the paper off the printing tile, not the other way around. Repeat so that there are lots of sheets to experiment with.

Wash everything up whilst the printing ink dries. Dab the printing block dry to avoid damage.

Add detail to the portrait by using the hard pencil to push down gently into the tile. These new cuts will now not print when you add the next colour, but remain light. This is a really effective way of depicting hair or clothes. Select the next lightest colour and repeat the printing process twice, using the pencil lines for guidance.

Leave to dry and display.

2.4 Hand sculptures

Aim

This is an activity that is really simple, but produces stunning results. The aim is for the young men to create 'sculptures' decorated to reflect their personalities.

You will need

- Modroc (strips of bandage pre-soaked in plaster of Paris) cut into 5cm-long strips
- Vaseline (petroleum jelly)
- scissors
- water
- plastic bowl
- gold or silver spray paint
- paint
- newspaper
- PVA/craft glue
- permanent markers.

How to do it

Ask for a volunteer who is prepared to have a hand 'sculpted' to demonstrate. Cover one hand thickly with Vaseline, making sure you coat his wrist and lower arm as well to stop the Modroc sticking to any hairs or skin.

Pour water into the plastic bowl and slowly soak a strip of plaster in the water. Immediately place this onto the volunteer's hand – it is best to start with the largest area first. Slowly cover the hand completely, including the fingers. Repeat several times to build up the sculpture. Once the hand is covered in at least four layers of Modroc wet your finger and go over the bandage, smoothing it flat.

Leave to dry; this will take about ten minutes, but may be longer if you have a lot of layers. You can tell when it is dry as it starts to peel away from the hand, usually from the fingers first.

You should have a perfect cast or 'sculpture' of the young man's hand. Divide the group into pairs so that they can take turns in creating sculptures. Once they are dry, the casts look really good sprayed gold or silver and decorated with tribal or tattoo designs, using paint and permanent markers.

When they are all completed invite everyone to share their sculpture, explaining design choices, and then display by pinning to the wall.

2.5 Welcome to my world

Aim

This collage is a good way to share information about personal likes and dislikes. The aim is to create a piece of visual art, without having to rely on drawing skills.

You will need

- a plain stretched canvas each (these are available cheaply at most DIY stores)
- a good selection of magazines
- scissors
- PVA glue or craft glue
- gems, sequins, glitter (optional).

How to do it

It is a good idea to make a collage of your own in advance to demonstrate. Start the session by showing this, explaining that it is representative of all the things that are important to you. Point out some of the meanings behind the images, explaining that the collage tells other people about who you are. I usually cut out letters to spell 'Welcome to my World' across mine.

Then, hand out magazines and scissors and invite the young men to look through them cutting out things that they like doing or aspire to doing. This can include things like sports, cars and music – in fact any dreams and ambitions are welcome, as well as things that remind them of family and friends. Photos can be added too.

Next, give a blank canvas to each participant with some glue. Explain that the task is to cover the canvas with images overlapping and merging.

Facilitate a group sharing time. Each young man can show their collage to introduce themselves and explain their choices.

Display the collages to remind each other until the group knows each other better.

2.6 Tell me about you...

Aim

This is probably the most traditional icebreaker ever! However, it is an ideal way to introduce group members to each other, particularly with young men who might find 'games' threatening.

You will need

- nothing!

How to do it

Ask the young men to choose a partner. This should be, where possible, someone that they do not already know. In turn the young men should tell each other three things about themselves. These can be unusual things, such as 'I keep pet snakes' or feelings, for example 'I find it really hard to control my temper sometimes.' Once each pair has finished, invite the young men to take it in turns to introduce their partner and share some of the discussions. Go around the group until everyone, including yourself and your co-worker, has been introduced.

2.7 Detectives

Aim

This icebreaker is good for mixed-ability groups as there is no reading or writing involved. It is really just a guessing game, but can be really good fun, encouraging the young men to interact.

You will need

- paper
- assorted pens
- an opaque bag.

How to do it

As each young man comes into the group session hand him a piece of paper and a pen.

Invite them to doodle, scribble or draw something. Stress that this is not an opportunity to spend ages on a piece of artwork, but something that should be done quickly. Encourage the young men to draw really intricate doodles so that no one will guess the artist! As they finish ask the young men to drop their papers into the bag. Shake well once all contributors have put their piece of paper into the bag.

Once everyone has placed his paper into the bag sit down in a circle. Each group member should then go up to the bag and take a paper out. If they pick out their own it should be replaced. The person who draws out the paper has first guess as to who drew it. Three guesses are allowed before the young man responsible confesses all!

Review the process – is it easy to guess? Do doodles and scribbles resemble the people who drew them? Are there any recurring themes?

2.8 Gingerbread men

Aim

The idea of this icebreaker is to encourage the boys or young men to consider what it is that they want from the group and the issues that are important to them. From this you can begin to discuss with them how they would like to use the time and amend your programme to reflect this.

You will need

- a large sheet of paper

- an assortment of felt pens or markers.

How to do it

Hand each young man a sheet of paper and some pens.

Ask each of them to draw a large gingerbread man in the middle of the paper. Explain that you are not looking for a perfect picture but a representation. If you are working with a group who you feel will struggle with this, simplify and ask them to draw a circle.

Now, ask the young men to write inside the gingerbread man all the things that they would like to get out of the time spent in the group. All ideas should be recorded in recognition that the young people may have different reasons for wanting to take part. For example, Eden may say, 'I want the opportunity to try out new activities,' but Joseph may have specific questions he wants answered and say, 'I want to find out what happens if you get arrested.'

Once all their ideas have been written inside the gingerbread man ask the young men to select a different colour pen. With this pen the young men should write down all the ideas they have for achieving the targets they have set themselves or noting things that they think would help with the issues that they have identified.

Once all the gingerbread men are complete, invite the group to share ideas and agree which things on the programme need to be added to or changed to meet the issues raised.

You can use this piece of work as part of the evaluation process later.

2.9 If I was ...

Aim

This is a non-threatening way for everyone in the group to introduce themselves and share information. You can change the topic to suit the age and interests of the group.

You will need

- nothing!

How to do it

Gather the young men together and ask them to form a circle. This means that you can all see each other and should be able to hear what is said.

Explain to the group that in order to begin to get to know each other you are going to ask each young man to say their name. As they do this, explain that you would like them to think about which type of animal they think best represents them and then share this too with their reasons. Ask the young men to consider their own personality and characteristics as well as how they look. For example, 'My name is Jed. If I was an animal I would be a panther as I think they are sleek, smooth and really fast!'

Go around the group so that each young man has a turn. It can be a good strategy for you to start the process off if there is any reluctance!

You can change the topic to anything that you think that the group will engage with. Suggestions include 'If I was...

- a car I would be...because...
- a colour I would be...because...
- a cartoon character I would be...because...'

Stop the game when everybody has had a turn and ask for any comments. Reflect on the animals chosen. Have the same animals been chosen? Ask the group to consider if these would be the same if the exercise asked for the group to choose for each other. For example, does everyone see Jed as a panther? Consider if choices were made based mainly on looks or skills and attributes.

2.10 Animals at the waterhole

This warm-up provides a safe environment for young men to explore self-image, whilst the fantasy element of the activity allows them to be open without exposing too much.

Aim

To begin to look at how individuals see themselves and discuss whether this differs from their public persona and how others perceive them.

You will need

- post-it notes
- pens
- a large sheet of paper with a blue pond or 'waterhole' drawn on.

How to do it

Place the sheet of paper with the pond drawn on it into the middle of the group. Explain to the young men that this is a waterhole. Go on to embellish your description by telling the group that this is the only waterhole for miles and all of the animals locally come here. Depending on your group you can be as creative as you like to build this part up.

Hand out a post-it note and pen to each group member. Ask them to think about which animal they would choose to represent themselves at the waterhole, and then write it on their piece of paper. Inform the volunteers that you are not asking them to put their names on their paper, but that you will be inviting them to talk about what they chose later.

Finally ask them to stick their post-it by the waterhole where they think that they should be.

When everybody has placed their 'animal' by the waterhole gather the group together to see what is there. Facilitate a discussion around what animals have been chosen. Which animal has been chosen most? Why? Invite individuals to share what they have chosen and the reasons why. For example, 'My name is Raj and I chose an eagle so that I can fly away and be free when I want.' Is this a surprise? How does this fit with how others see Raj in the group? Does it fit with the image he projects?

2.11 Pack of cards

This is a good way of randomly dividing the young men into groups. The only catch is that you will need a reasonable idea of how many are going to turn up to the session or it will not work out!

Aim

To divide the large group into smaller groups.

You will need

- a deck of playing cards.

How to do it

Before your group arrives sort out the cards into suits. Then work out how many young men you are expecting and divide the number by four. This will give you the number of cards you need from each suit. For example, if you are expecting 16 young men to attend the group you will need to shuffle together the ace, two, three and four of each suit. If the group is much smaller just use diamonds and spades or hearts and clubs to obtain the same result.

To divide the group, shuffle the cards and ask each young man to take one. Stress that they should not look at it but should hold it face outwards in front of them. You can ask them to hold it on their foreheads if you think they will go with it!

When everyone has a card in their hand ask them to find their suit without speaking! This starts the communication process as the young men have to work together to get into the correct groups. A variation on this is to ask the young people to sort themselves into same-number groups, that is, all the aces together, etc.

Once they have 'found' the rest of their group you can start!

2.12 Picture postcards

Aim

This is another 'sorting game' which involves participants working together to create small groups of three to work in.

You will need

- a good selection of postcards
- scissors.

How to do it

If you want to use this method it is a good idea to start collecting as many postcards as possible! Postcards raising awareness of issues for young people, such as those published by local health promotion teams, sexual health clinics or organisations supporting young people are usually free and easily available. They can also be a conversation starter or provoke discussion.

Once you have your great selection of well-designed, young-people-friendly cards – cut each one into three! You will need one piece for each group member. If you know that this will not work out with the number of young men in your group, either cut one card into four or cut one in half so that no one is left out.

Start the session by forming a circle and lay the cards out randomly face down in the middle of the group. Ask each young man to go into the middle, pick up a card and return to the circle. When everyone has a card in their hand, set them the task of finding the pieces to complete their postcard.

Once everyone has achieved this, the group should have sub-divided itself into small groups that they can now work in.

2.13 Perfect pairs

This is a good way to divide the group into pairs. If you know that the group do not like reading activities consider making a set of cards with picture pairs to find.

Aim

To provide opportunities for the group to interact as they find their 'pair'.

You will need

- a set of 'pairs cards'
- a few spare cards in case you have too many young people and have to improvise.

How to do it

Shuffle the cards and ask each young man to choose one. If you have an odd number in the group use one of the blanks to make up another card along one of the themes, for example 'footballer', 'coach' and 'referee'.

Invite everyone to look at their card, but ask them not to tell anybody else what is written on it. It does not matter if you have duplicate 'pairs', so long as each person can find a partner.

Ask the young men to go off and 'find' their pair. They can only do this by asking indirect questions; for example, they cannot ask, 'Are you a nurse?', but can ask, 'Do you work in a hospital?'

Once everyone has found the card that corresponds to their own explain that their 'pair' will now be their partner for the next activity.

PAIRS CARDS

Singer	Fan	Artist	Model
Nurse	Patient	Teacher	Pupil
Parent	Child	Policeman	Criminal
Actor	Audience	Sales Assistant	Customer
Footballer	Coach	Taxi Driver	Passenger
Spaceman	Alien	DJ	Dancer
		Boss	Worker

2.14 Movie cards

This is the final idea along this theme! The activity encourages the young men to start talking, but you will need to make sure that the cards you use are the names of movies that the group are likely to have heard of. This is not the opportunity to show off your knowledge of rare French films!

Aim

This is another way to divide the group into random pairs.

You will need

- a set of the 'movie cards'
- a few spare cards in case you have too many young people and have to improvise
- small envelopes.

How to do it

Make a set of cards that have the titles of popular movies on. Put half the title on one card and the other half on another, for example 'Mary' and 'Poppins'. Make sure that these are age appropriate and likely to be familiar to the young men. Place a card in each envelope and seal unlabelled.

As the group arrives hand an envelope to each young man, asking them not to open it until you say so.

If you know you have an odd number in the group choose a movie title that can easily be broken down into three pieces, for example 'Blair' 'Witch' 'Project' and make a set of cards.

Once everyone has arrived and been given an envelope, invite everyone to look at their card, but ask them not to tell anybody else what is written on it. Ask the young men to go off and 'find' the card that makes up the title of their film. They can only do this by asking indirect questions; for example, 'Are you a horror film?'

Once everyone has found the card that corresponds to their own explain that their 'pair' will now be their partner for the next activity.

MOVIE CARDS

Lord of	the Rings
Star	Wars
The Wizard	of Oz
Willy Wonka	and the Chocolate Factory
Harry Potter	and the Half-Blood Prince
Slumdog	Millionaire
Indiana Jones	and the Temple of Doom
Gold	finger

2.15 Anagrams

Aim

This has the dual purpose of dividing the young men into small groups, as well as offering the opportunity to find out members' names if you are working with a new group.

You will need

- A6 paper (approx 4 × 6") in different colours (you need enough of each colour to divide the group up equally, so for 20 young men you could use five colours and make four cards of each)

- glue

- a marker.

How to do it

In advance of the session get a list of all the young men's names; otherwise it won't work! Take a piece of paper and using the marker devise an anagram of the first young person's name. For example, Alexander becomes 'RAXLNEADE'. Repeat, using different coloured paper until you have one for each member of the group. Make sure you have a couple of spare cards made up and left blank ready to do if you get extra participants!

When the group arrive seat them in a circle and ask them to say their names one at a time. Next, hand out the cards having shuffled them fully first so that each card is handed out at random.

When everyone has a card set them the task of going around the room and talking to each other until they find the card with the anagram of their name on. Stress that they need to talk with each other to find their card, not just grab the card and look!

Explain that they will now work in a group with those who have the same colour card. You now have the group divided and ready for the main activity!

2.16 Dot pairs

Aim

This is a really quick and easy way to divide a group up into pairs. It does not take long to do, encourages non-verbal communication and is appropriate for all age and ability groups.

You will need

- a good selection of coloured self-adhesive dots.

How to do it

Making sure that the young men cannot see what colour you are using, stick a coloured 'dot' on each group member's forehead. If you think that this will not be appropriate with this group, you may want to vary this and stick the dots on their backs.

Explain to the young men that the task you are setting them is to find a partner from within the group who has the same colour sticker on them without speaking! Allow five to ten minutes (depending on the size of the group) for the young men to sort themselves into pairs. Make sure that you facilitate this carefully to ensure that no one cheats!

Once the task is complete reflect on the process with the group. How hard was it to do this without speaking? What helped? What have they learnt about non-verbal communication? What other situations may they use this in?

Chapter 3

Developing Communication Skills

3.1 Advertising me

Aim

This session aims to increase self-esteem and celebrate positive personality traits.

You will need

- magazines
- scissors
- glue
- A3 paper (approx 11 × 17")
- markers.

How to do it

Introduce the session by asking the young men to consider the purpose of advertising. Talk about the methods used to get the message across – visually and with words. Explain that ads promote the positive aspects of a product to persuade the public to buy it.

The task for each young man is to come up with an advertisement persuading someone to become his friend. The advert should depict positive aspects of themselves through pictures, words, or a combination of the two. Hand out markers, glue, scissors and magazines plus a sheet of paper each.

If anyone has a difficult time thinking of reasons someone would want to be their friend, suggest some prompts, such as loyalty, trust or sense of humour.

At the end of the session take turns to share advertisements, encouraging members of the group to confirm the positive qualities of the presenter.

3.2 Making my voice heard

Aim

This activity aims to prepare young men for taking part in discussions and considers appropriate behaviour and turn-taking.

You will need

- copies of the 'making my voice heard sheet'
- pens.

How to do it

Start the session by suggesting that taking part in discussions where people are talking about their feelings or things that they feel strongly about can be difficult. This is particularly so if you don't agree with what is being said, or have a point that you really want to make. Point out that people are far less likely to listen to the ideas of someone who is shouting, aggressive or talking over others, and more likely to listen to someone who makes their point assertively, respectfully and clearly. Suggest that one way to make sure you say what you need to whilst respecting the rights of everyone else can be to prepare first. If you know in advance points that you want to raise you are less likely to forget something that is important to you or get distracted during a discussion.

Share copies of the 'making my voice heard sheet' around the group with pens. Invite the young men to think about points that they really want to make and then follow through the process outlined.

Facilitate a short discussion picking up on some of the ideas recorded, particularly about how what is said can impact on others. Use during the next sessions as appropriate.

MAKING MY VOICE HEARD SHEET

Name	Possible ideas	How could I raise this?
What is it you want to say?		
Who does this issue affect?		
How does it make you feel?		
How do you think other people will feel?		
Have you any other concerns about this?		

3.3 Active listening

Aim

This game quickly demonstrates the need for active listening to be able to complete a task.

You will need

- one picture that is very simple, for example a photo of a classical building
- one picture that is complicated, for example an abstract photo of a building
- pencils
- sheets of plain paper each.

How to do it

Make photocopies of each picture so that there are enough for each member of the group.

Ask the young men to work in pairs and hand out pencils to everyone. Ask them to sit on chairs back to back so that they can't see each other's face.

Now, for each pair give a copy of Picture 1 to one young man and a copy of Picture 2 to the other. Stress that they should not show each other what they are looking at or it won't work! Explain that in turn they are going to describe their own picture to their partner, who will then draw what they hear. Each round will take three minutes. Keep time and increase pressure by stepping up time checks as the time passes the two-minute mark.

Once each person has had their turn at drawing and describing stop the activity and invite the young men to show each other the pictures they were given, and compare it to what they drew. How close are they?

As a whole group review the process. Which picture was easier to draw? Who gave really good instructions and how? What instructions were hard to understand? What listening skills were required? How did the time constraints add to the pressure? Why? Make the point that it is easier to describe something that you can see clearly and know, and that it is easier to listen to and act on an instruction you understand fully. It can be really frustrating for both the listener and the communicator to try to describe concepts or ideas that aren't familiar. Make a list of the key skills the young men think are important for good communication to refer back to. These should include:

- speaking clearly, using language that is understood

- using points of reference to aid understanding

- facing the person so they can see non-verbal communication

- leaving space for questions or time to check out understanding

- actively listening.

3.4 Effective communication

Aim

This activity uses a range of communication skills to achieve a group task. It highlights the need for clear instructions and good listening skills as well as developing non-verbal communication.

You will need

- a scarf or mask
- a set of written instructions
- props (related to the tasks you choose).

How to do it

To prepare for the activity, devise a short set of instructions for a simple task and collect the props required for it. For example, 'Direct the Listener to put on the hat, sit on the chair and pour a cup of water, then drink it!' For this task you would need a chair, a hat, a glass, a jug of water and a cup. You can choose as many tasks as you like, of varying levels of difficulty, depending on the time you have and the needs of the group.

Ask the young men to select the group member that they think is the best listener. Bring him forward and ask him to stand 20 paces away from the rest of the group. Turn the 'Listener' to face the group, but place the scarf or mask over his eyes so that he can't see. Explain that as the group Listener he is not allowed to speak again until the game is over. He is also not to move unless told to do so.

Now, ask the young men to select their best communicator. Invite this young man to step forward and take ten paces, before stopping. He should then turn and face the group and the Listener. The 'Communicator' is allowed to speak.

The rest of the group needs to stand to the side of the Communicator, so he can see them, but maintain the distance between them and the Listener. After this point the main group may not say anything to either the Listener or the Communicator until the activity is over.

Now produce the props and a set of written instructions, and give these to the group. Only they are allowed to see them.

Without speaking, the group now has to make the Communicator understand the directions so that he can tell the Listener what to do. The young men in the main group can only use non-verbal communication; mouthing or whispering words is not allowed!

Once the task is complete congratulate everyone on their achievement and review the process. What made it easier or harder? Which communication skills were required for this to be successful? Did anyone lead the way? Did everyone participate? Pull out the main learning points.

3.5 Body language game

Aim

This is a short role-play game that introduces the idea of non-verbal communication.

You will need

- a copy of the 'body language cards'.

How to do it

Seat the young men in a semi-circle, with one chair in the middle facing the group. Open the session with a short discussion about how non-verbal communication shows others how we are feeling or behaving without any words being spoken. Suggest that sometimes people get into conflict because they miss someone's signals, or don't read them correctly. Ask the young men to consider how true this is and to think about their own body language. Does this change when you are happy or when you feel really angry about something?

Next, ask for a volunteer to demonstrate this. Introduce the set of cards you have and the game. Tell the group that whilst one young man is seated in the middle of the circle 'acting out' what is on his card, the others can ask questions to try to guess what it is. Questions should be answered in character, but the word on the card must not be used. So, for example, if the card says 'angry', it is fine to reply to all questions in a grumpy, confrontational way, as long as the word 'angry' isn't actually said.

A guess can be made at any stage in the process. If it is correct then the young man who guessed takes a new card, swaps seats and begins again. If the guess is wrong continue until someone gets it right. Try to keep the questions moving along so that the game keeps pace. The game ends when everyone has had a go at being in the middle.

BODY LANGUAGE CARDS

ANGRY	SHY
EMBARRASSED	HAPPY
OFFENDED	CONFIDENT
MISUNDERSTOOD	SAD
EXCITED	DISTRACTED
NERVOUS	BORED
DISGUSTED	TIRED
SURPRISED	FRIGHTENED

3.6 Living at home

This exercise works on the basis that wherever you live there are 'rules'. If you live at home your parents usually set these, but renting or flat-sharing has its own share of rules that the group may not have considered!

Aim

The main aim of this session is to share experiences and discuss potential areas of conflict and begin to develop strategies to negotiate or accept them.

You will need

- small slips of paper

- pens

- contact numbers for local support groups and social services.

How to do it

Begin the session with a short discussion about what the word 'home' means. Is it just a place to sleep and store your CDs? Does it mean more? Why?

Then hand out the slips of paper and pens. Ask the young men to individually consider the good and bad things about living with parents or carers.

When they have thought about it, ask the young men to use three slips of paper to write:

1. the five best things about living at home

2. the five worst things about living at home

3. five things that they would do differently if they lived away from home.

Once the group has completed the task ask them to stick their notes in three separate piles. They do not have to put their names on them.

Ask for a volunteer from the group to read out the 'best things'. Are there similarities? For example, how many said 'I get my washing done' or 'My mum's Sunday dinner!' Discuss suggestions and encourage the young men to enlarge upon what they have said.

Invite another volunteer to go through the same process with the 'worst things'. These are usually the 'rules' of the house, for example, 'Whilst you live under my roof you have to be in by 10 o'clock on a school night!' It is often these imposed or non-negotiable conditions that are the source of real tension in the home. What are the major areas of conflict? Be aware that some of the young men may have experiences they find difficult or painful to talk about and take the opportunity to remind the group of any confidentiality agreements, including your own boundaries. Make sure that you have the numbers of a child helpline (e.g. ChildLine in the UK, or Childhelp USA in the US), social services or your local youth counselling centre available. It is also a good idea to have information about the legalities regarding young people living away from home, including those in the care of the local authority.

Then look at the pile of things that would be done differently. Review these in the same way as the other notes, but additionally challenge or question the practicalities involved in achieving the wish list. For example, how realistic is it to say 'I would play my music as loud as I want, whenever I want'? Question if this would be possible, unless they are planning to live on an uninhabited desert island!

Invite the young men to look again at the wish list and discuss if there is any way that a compromise could be worked towards that would enable some of the 'worst' things to be resolved or agreed. For example, for the young man who gets 'told off' for coming in late at night there could be a type of contract between him and his parent that he will phone if he is going to be late.

Depending on the group you can work through each of the negative points to see if they could be reframed to become more acceptable to the young person and his parent or use ideas from all three piles as a discussion framework.

Agree with the young men to each work on one area raised during the session for the next week and suggest that you review how the tactics worked (or didn't!) when you meet again.

3.7 Who is confident?

Aim

This group activity uses well-known male celebrities as a discussion prompt and asks young men to assess their own levels of confidence.

You will need

- pictures of male celebrities cut out of magazines
- flipchart and marker
- Blu-Tack.

How to do it

Divide the young men into small groups and hand each a selection of pictures of celebrities. These can be sporting heroes, music stars, actors or politicians – it doesn't really matter what they are famous for; they just need to be recognisable to the young men.

Each group should discuss their pictures considering the following questions:

1. Which of these celebrities do you think is confident?

2. How do they show they are confident?

3. Which aren't? How do they behave?

Draw a continuum on a sheet of flipchart paper marked 'Confident' at one end and 'Not confident' at the other.

Now, in rotation invite each group to choose a celebrity and share the conclusions reached before sticking them onto the continuum where they think they should go. Encourage discussion as each celebrity is placed onto the board. Finally, invite each young man to place themselves between the 'Confident' and 'Not confident' poles.

3.8 Yes/no game

This is a well-known game that relies on quick thinking and effective communication skills.

Aim

The aim of this game is to answer questions without saying 'yes' or 'no' for 30 seconds. It is a lot harder than it sounds!

You will need

- a stopwatch.

How to do it

Nominate a young man to go first. If the group are reluctant, start the game off by having a go yourself and asking one of the young men to time you.

Start by asking easy questions, for example 'What is your name?' 'Does everyone call you that?' etc. Keep the speed up, as it is easier to think of alternatives to yes/ no with long pauses. You can increase the tension by having time checks called out every ten seconds or saying things like 'Are you sure about that?' The first young man to achieve the 30 seconds gets to ask the questions next!

Rotate who holds the stopwatch and encourage the rest of the group to support the person answering questions. You can keep going as long as the group wants to!

3.9 Leadership self-assessment

Aim

This self-assessment is a good way to start work around leadership and teamwork. It enables young men to reflect on their own qualities and consider skills that they would like to develop or build on.

You will need

- flipchart and markers
- copies of the 'leadership self-assessment sheet'
- pens.

How to do it

Start the session off by inviting the young men to tell you what qualities or personal attributes are needed to be a great leader. Try to look beyond physical attributes, for example, action heroes might be strong and tough, but is that enough to get others to follow them? Encourage them to share any heroes that they have and record ideas on the flipchart paper.

Now, hand each participant a 'leadership self-assessment sheet' and a pen. Ask that everyone fill theirs in, but stress that as this is a self-assessment they should try to be honest; otherwise it will not have any meaning. Inform the group that you won't be asking them to share how they score themselves on individual questions but will be discussing overall scores later.

Once all the young men have completed their assessment and added up their scores, bring the group back together for a discussion. Invite the young men to comment on their scores, for example whether they think they are a fair reflection of their leadership skills. Raise the following points for consideration:

- Are some people 'born' leaders?
- In order to be able to give instructions do you need to be able to take them too?
- How do you show respect to all if you are a group leader?
- How can you motivate people to follow you?

Move on to consider, either as a whole group or on individual action plans, what additional skills need building on to develop strong leadership skills. Use these to plan additional sessions and create opportunities to try out skills.

LEADERSHIP SELF-ASSESSMENT SHEET

This survey provides feedback about your feelings about leading others. Rate yourself on a scale of one to five, with one being a definite YES and five being a definite NO. Be honest about your answers as this is only for your own self-assessment.

	YES				NO
I enjoy working in teams.	1	2	3	4	5
I am able to speak confidently to others.	1	2	3	4	5
I am good at planning,	1	2	3	4	5
I can understand rules and communicate them to others.	1	2	3	4	5
I feel comfortable asking people for advice.	1	2	3	4	5
I am good at problem-solving.	1	2	3	4	5

	YES				NO
I am good at instructing others.	1	2	3	4	5
I am good at motivating others to do their best.	1	2	3	4	5
I am effective at sorting out arguments.	1	2	3	4	5
I generally do what I say I will.	1	2	3	4	5
I enjoy getting feedback from others about myself.	1	2	3	4	5
I am really good at listening to others.	1	2	3	4	5
If I make a mistake, I admit it and try to put it right.	1	2	3	4	5
I am honest and trustworthy.	1	2	3	4	5

	YES				NO
I value diversity and can show people respect.	1	2	3	4	5
I like leading others.	1	2	3	4	5

Score the survey by adding up the numbers that you circled.

60 or more

A score of 60 or more indicates that you feel comfortable taking the lead and that you have many of the qualities required to be effective. Consider how as a leader you can encourage others to follow you, and also how good your team skills are when it is your turn to follow!

40 to 59

You have many leadership qualities, but may not always choose to take the lead or feel confident taking that role. Have a think about which skills you would like to develop further to raise your confidence so that when it is your turn to lead, you shine!

40 or less

A score of 40 or less indicates a general dislike of wanting to lead or a perceived inability to perform the tasks required of a leader. If your prefer being part of a team rather than leading it consider how assertive you are about making your wishes and feelings known. Good leaders should take everyone's views into account so make sure you have the skills to be heard!

3.10 The bus stop

Aim

This is a drama-based activity designed to encourage the young men to practise their communication skills to formulate arguments and be assertive. It works best if the group know each other enough to be confident in arguing their case!

You will need

- nothing!

How to do it

Explain to the young men that this game revolves around a group of strangers waiting to catch a bus.

Ask the group to nominate one young man to be the 'bus driver'. This should not be a worker as your role will be to facilitate what happens within the group. You may want to manage this process so that someone can experience the leadership role of bus driver who normally does not get the opportunity.

The rest of the young men stand in a line, representing a bus queue. Suggest that they formulate a character for themselves that explains why they are in the bus queue. This can be anyone of any gender or age that they want! If they are looking doubtful, offer a few ideas, for example a man with a broken leg, a man late for a meeting, a student on their way back from college.

The bus driver pulls up and says to the queue, 'One place, and one place only.' Each person in the queue then needs to present the reason why they should have the last place on the bus! Encourage the young men to be creative with the reasons they use to tell the bus driver why they need the place. For example, the man late for a meeting may be in danger of losing his job if he doesn't get there! Remind them throughout the process that the final choice lies with the bus driver and only he says who gets the seat.

Once the decision has been made talk the experience through with the group. Did they think it was a good decision? What else could they have said to alter the bus driver's mind? How did it feel to have one person making the decision?

3.11 Tamus Square

Aim

This is a problem-solving activity that demonstrates the need for effective communication.

You will need

- chalk

- post-it notes with the numbers one to eight written on them for each team.

How to do it

To prepare for the activity, draw two chalk grids on the ground, marking two vertical lines with two horizontal lines equally crossing them. You should have nine squares that look like a noughts and crosses grid. If you have a very large group, draw up several of these 'Tamus Squares'.

Divide the young men into two (or more) teams. Ask for eight volunteers from each team and hand them a post-it note with a concealed number on each; stress that they should keep their number a secret.

Now, the task is for each group of eight to arrange itself on the grid in numerical order, moving only when their number is called. Other members of their team can shout out instructions and help in any way apart from physically moving them. When one team achieves correct alignment, stop.

This time, the task is for eight young men from each team to achieve the same task but in silence. They can only use non-verbal communication and are not allowed help from other team-mates. Again, stop as soon as one team manages to solve the problem.

Finally, do the same puzzle, this time designating a team leader for each eight. The rest of the team should follow his instructions; no additional help is allowed from the rest of the team

Review the entire process, encouraging feedback from team members who observed. What helped solve this puzzle? What blocked people working together effectively?

Chapter 4

Expressing Emotions

4.1 Understanding assertiveness

Aim

This is essentially a sorting game based on attitudes and values, rather than knowledge, which encourages young men to develop their understanding of assertiveness.

You will need

- a set of the 'assertiveness cards'
- scissors.

How to do it

Copy and cut up the assertiveness cards and shuffle them. Introduce the session by asking for a definition of the word 'assertiveness'. Explain that this can be mistaken for 'aggressiveness' and agree what the differences are.

Divide the large group into three and hand a set of assertiveness cards to each. Set the groups the task of selecting nine cards out of the set that they think offer the best descriptions of being assertive.

Now, ask the groups to make a diamond shape with the nine cards they have chosen, 'ranking' their selection. So, the card that they think best explains assertiveness should form the top of the diamond, the next two cards go below this and so on to form a diamond shape. Those cards that they think can be true sometimes or may only apply in certain situations should be placed towards the bottom of the diamond.

When the young men have completed the task, ask them to leave their group diamond nines in place and review each set in turn. Invite them to share some of their own experiences, for example a time when it was difficult to be assertive or where they needed courage to say what they wanted or felt.

Conclude that even the most confident person can find it hard to be assertive in some circumstances and agree priority areas for future sessions.

ASSERTIVENESS CARDS

Assertiveness is all about being popular so people do as you tell them.	Being assertive is the same as being cocky.	Being assertive means not listening to anyone else's ideas but your own.
Being assertive means saying what you think in a way that is respectful to others.	Being assertive means that you are brave enough to stand up for yourself.	To be assertive you have to give your opinion forcefully.
Assertiveness is not changing your mind just to go along with people.	Assertiveness is expressing yourself confidently but not angrily.	Assertiveness means persuading other people to have the same opinion as you.
Assertiveness is being aggressively confident.	To be assertive you have to be prepared to argue.	Assertiveness is about making other people do what you want them to.

4.2 How assertive are you?

Aim

This quick quiz outlines a range of situations where assertiveness may be required and enables young men to begin to assess their own skills.

You will need

- copies of the '"How assertive are you?" quiz'
- pens.

How to do it

Hand out a pen and a copy of the quiz to each young man. If you know that some group members will struggle with this suggest working in pairs.

Introduce the quiz. You want the group to look at each statement and tick if they think the statement is true or place a cross in the box if they disagree. The idea is to tick the statements that are closest to their own reaction in a similar circumstance.

Once everyone has finished, ask the group to come together. Read out the statements one at a time, inviting the young men to say whether they ticked the statements or not. Encourage discussion and ask them to share examples of situations where they have had similar experiences.

Finally, reflect with the group on the statements that have the most ticks. Do these statements show assertive or more passive behaviour? Encourage the young men to discuss what the difference is and conclude that most people feel more assertive and less assertive in different areas of their lives.

Move on to consider ways of becoming more assertive without becoming aggressive.

'HOW ASSERTIVE ARE YOU?' QUIZ

Please have a look at the statements below. If you think the statement is true then place a tick in the box; if you think that it is false then place a cross.

I often get my way when debating with others.	
I usually keep it to myself when someone annoys me.	
I feel guilty if I raise my voice or speak forcefully to someone.	
I have no difficulty saying 'no' to people.	
I only speak up for myself when I get upset.	
I try hard to please others, even putting their needs before mine.	
I often say 'sorry' before disagreeing with someone.	
I usually say something if someone crosses my personal boundaries.	
I tend to give in and do what others want.	

4.3 Passive/assertive/aggressive

Aim

This session offers the opportunity to explore passive, aggressive and assertive behaviour and consider alternative ways of expressing feelings.

You will need

- a flipchart sheet with a drawing of a thermometer on it
- post-it notes and pens.

How to do it

Divide the main group into threes. Ask each small group to discuss male characters in soap operas or well-known films and the way that the actors portray feeling angry. Encourage them to think in particular about behaviour and consequences. Then hand out post-it notes to each group and ask them to write the name of a soap or film character on each one. Good examples of very visually angry characters are Robert de Niro in *Taxi Driver* and Jack Nicholson in *As Good as it Gets*.

Now, show the young men the anger thermometer drawing you have put on the wall. Explain that the thermometer is a continuum, with 'passive' at one end of the scale, through 'assertive' to 'aggressive' at the far end. Offer these broad definitions to help:

- Passive: Not expressing your own feelings or saying nothing.
- Aggressive: Asking for what you want or saying how you feel in an offensive, threatening or angry way.
- Assertive: Asking for what you want or saying how you feel in an honest and respectful way that does not infringe on another person's safety, dignity or well-being.

Next, invite a member from each group in turn to place their soap or film character onto the thermometer in the place that they think best defines the character's behaviours. Encourage the young men to explain their decisions and ask them if they think the character gets what they want as a result of their behaviour. Go on to consider alternative ways in which they could reach a positive conclusion.

Finally, hand each group member a small post-it note, ask him to write his name on it and then stick it onto the anger thermometer in the place that they think reflects their behaviour best.

4.4 Assertiveness quiz

Aim

To look at the differences between being 'assertive', 'passive' and 'aggressive' and provoke discussion within the group.

You will need

- copies of the 'assertiveness quiz'
- pens.

How to do it

Hand out a pen and a copy of the quiz to each young man. Explain that they should complete this alone, but if you know that some group members will struggle with this suggest working in pairs.

Introduce the quiz by saying that there a series of situations shown on the page. You want the group to look and tick the response that they feel would be closest to their own reaction in a similar circumstance.

Once everyone has finished ask the young men to add up their scores and gather them together to facilitate a feedback session. Use the suggested score and definitions below to reflect on their answers.

Assertive, passive and aggressive quiz scores

The higher your score the more assertive you are!

Assertive behaviour includes:

- expressing your true thoughts or beliefs clearly, without shouting
- asking for what you want in a way that is honest, but respectful of other people
- feeling in control of what you say and do
- standing up for your rights with dignity
- making your own decisions and taking responsibility for them.

Passive behaviour includes:

- going along with other people, even if you don't agree with them
- saying nothing

- not standing up for yourself or what you think is right

- not telling others what you think, want or believe

- playing a 'victim' role

- not making your own decisions or taking personal responsibility.

Aggressive behaviour includes:

- getting what you want at all costs, regardless of others

- shouting and being aggressive to someone if they don't agree with you

- trying to force other people to do what you want

- putting people down to make you look better

- bullying

- humiliating or embarrassing someone

- threatening physical or emotional harm.

Finally see who has the highest scores in the group. Do they see themselves as assertive? Invite the young men to share their experiences of being assertive and getting their voices heard. How easy is it to say what you want? Encourage them to consider situations where perhaps they thought they were being assertive, but it was mistaken for aggression. Similarly a time when they responded passively and went along with something they didn't really want to do. Finally, consider ways that they can practise being assertive and set some personal goals.

ASSERTIVENESS QUIZ

		Always Score 4	Mostly Score 3	Not always Score 2	Never Score 1
1.	When someone compliments you, do you know what to say?				
2.	If someone asks to borrow something you don't want to lend can you say no?				
3.	Do you ask questions if you don't understand?				
4.	Do you admit to making mistakes?				
5.	Do you feel confident when you say what you think?				
6.	When someone puts pressure on you to do something you know to be wrong do you do it?				
7.	Do you stick up for other people?				
8.	If your friends said something you didn't agree with would you say that you disagreed?				
9.	Do you apologise if you are wrong?				
10.	Do you find it easy to ask for help?				
	TOTAL IN EACH COLUMN				

4.5 That makes me angry!

Aim

This is a tool to help young men identify their own anger triggers, so that they can go on to learn more positive ways of expressing themselves.

You will need

- copies of the '"That makes me angry!" sheet'
- pens
- flipchart and markers.

How to do it

Start any session looking at anger by reinforcing the fact that anger is an emotion as justified as any other and that everyone feels angry at some point. Make sure that they realise that anger sessions are not about suppressing feelings or telling people that it is wrong to be angry, but more about finding different ways to express themselves. This includes identifying personal anger triggers, which is what this activity aims to do.

Hand out a '"That makes me angry!" sheet' and a pen to each group member. At this stage you want them to be completed individually, but if you are working with a group with low literacy skills consider doing the whole session as a group exercise.

Once the young men have completed their sheets, go through the sheet asking for a show of hands after each point so that you can pick out the most popular anger triggers for discussion. Additionally, pick up on any that are clearly a big issue for individual members. Encourage the young men to think about how a particular trigger makes them feel, and how this leads on to how it makes them behave.

Divide the group into pairs and ask the young men to discuss a time when they got angry, how they felt, what they did and the consequences of their behaviour. Have them think about the point at which they could have stopped, and what process they went through to make decisions – good or bad.

Facilitate a discussion that considers what they could do differently, now that they have identified personal triggers, to avoid any negative consequences. Record everyone's ideas on the flipchart to follow up in future sessions.

'THAT MAKES ME ANGRY!' SHEET

Have a look through the following and tick those that you consider personal anger triggers:

- ☐ When someone tells me lies
- ☐ Someone not believing me when I am telling the truth
- ☐ Someone borrowing my things and not giving them back
- ☐ When someone says things about my family
- ☐ Someone shouting at me when I don't think I deserve it
- ☐ When someone pushes/touches me
- ☐ My favourite team losing an important game
- ☐ My ex going out with someone else
- ☐ People not listening to me
- ☐ When someone interrupts me
- ☐ Someone turning over the TV when I want to see something else
- ☐ People not doing what they say they will
- ☐ When other people are angry
- ☐ When I feel embarrassed
- ☐ Bullying
- ☐ Giving up a habit (e.g. smoking)
- ☐ Not winning in a game
- ☐ Being physically threatened
- ☐ Being blamed for something I didn't do

4.6 Anger: think, feel, do

Aim

This session offers young men a range of scenarios that may trigger anger and encourages them to think through the potential consequences of actions taken.

You will need

- to enlarge and copy the 'anger scenarios sheet' and then cut it up.

How to do it

Seat the young men in a circle, so that everyone is facing each other. Explain that you are going to hand each of them in turn a card with a scenario on it. They should read it, and then imagine what they would think, feel and finally do if it was happening to them. For example, if you spend days preparing for a job that you don't get offered you might:

- THINK that the person who interviewed you didn't like you and favoured someone else

- FEEL bad about yourself and embarrassed that you didn't get the job

- DO shout at them that you didn't want to work for them anyway!

Then invite the rest of the group to consider what the consequences of any decision might be. So in the example above, a consequence might be that not only do you feel really down and unhappy, but you also can't apply for any more jobs at that company as you were rude to the boss. Keep reminding the young men that we all have different triggers and ways of coping with situations that make us angry and that no one way is right. Go on to encourage suggestions for other ways to cope with the situations given. For example, if you don't get a job it is perfectly reasonable to ask the person who interviewed you for feedback so that you can improve your interview skills for next time.

At the next session, invite the young men to share any times that they have felt angry since you last met and go through the same think, feel, do process. Suggest that it is really useful if you can use this model as a tool to work through real life events and stresses as it enables you to consider consequences and make positive choices.

ANGER SCENARIOS SHEET

You spend days preparing for a job interview and then don't get it.	You are confused about your sexuality, and all your friends make fun of 'gays'.
People laugh at you for the colour of your hair.	Your brother borrows your new shirt without asking and when you put it on you discover a cigarette burn.
Your mum pays for your younger brother's school trip, but refuses to help pay for your holiday. She says you should pay because you work.	You are in a club and have a big row with your friend. Door staff throw you out for raising your voice but let your mate stay.
Your team loses and fans of the opposition are chanting and saying your team is rubbish.	A boy at school calls your mum a 'whore'.
Your best mate goes off with your girlfriend.	Someone breaks into your car and steals your sound system.
The college threatens to chuck you off your course because you have had too much time off.	A teacher makes fun of you in front of the class and your mates laugh.

4.7 Chain argument

This activity comes with a warning! Although it offers the young men a forum to experience controlled arguments and compliments in equal measure you need to be very careful at setting and maintaining boundaries so that it does not become an opportunity for destructive comments and bullying.

Aim

To encourage the young men to reflect on the process that leads to conflict and also that which produces compliments. The idea is for the young people to decide whether it is easier to criticise others or to see their good points. There is no wrong or right answer as it is personal and up for discussion!

You will need

- nothing!

How to do it

Designate an area as a 'stage'. Explain to the young men that the object of the activity is to experience conflict and compliments and then discuss what feels the most comfortable to both give and receive. Try to give an idea of the exercise without giving too much away to avoid the group becoming reserved about what they do.

Set some ground rules:

1. Any conversation that takes place ends when the young man comes off stage.

2. Any 'argument' must be abstract and not a continuation of any outside grievance or vendetta!

3. Only two people can be on stage at any one time and the dialogue will only take place for as long as they want – at any time they can withdraw and the next person can have a go.

4. If the experience becomes uncomfortable at any time the group should stop and review what is going on.

They can then add to these if they wish.

Invite two young men to begin. Explain that one should stand on the 'stage' whilst the next one approaches them and begins an 'argument'. If there is reluctance or uncertainty about doing this demonstrate what you mean by starting off the process with your co-worker. Be sure to make it clear that this should not be too personal. A good example is to begin with something that may be emotive but not too sensitive: 'So why do you support Manchester United then, they're rubbish.' You should then carry on until one person has had enough and leaves the 'stage'.

The next young man joins the remaining group member on the stage and begins a new 'argument'. If at any time this looks to be getting too personal – stop!

When everybody has had an opportunity to participate ask the group to begin the process again, only this time instead of picking an argument with someone they need to compliment or say something positive about them. Once again this will need to be managed carefully.

At the end of the process discuss with the young men how they felt. What was easier? Arguing or complimenting? What felt the most comfortable, the giving or receiving of either? Remember to stress that there is no right or wrong here. You may be surprised at the answers!

4.8 Wall of anger

Aim

The aim of this activity is to provide one huge wall of painting to visualise 'anger' and represent the emotion in colour and words to which each member of the group has contributed.

You will need

- large rolls of paper
- pots of paint
- brushes
- masking tape
- whistle
- watch or clock
- old shirts or T-shirts for everyone.

How to do it

Before the young men arrive, prepare the space using the rolls of paper cut and taped to cover the entire wall space floor to ceiling. You could also include the floor space if you are feeling adventurous!

Start the session off by introducing the idea that colours and images can represent feelings and emotions. Go on to talk about word association and how different words can spark different mental pictures in each of us. You may want to give an example here! Ask the group to close their eyes and think about the word 'cold'. What colours come to mind?

Once the young men have grasped the idea ask them to think about the word 'anger' and what it looks like to them. Ask them to try to visualise a time when they felt really angry and hold on to the ideas and colours that flash into their heads.

Now, hand each young man a pot of paint and a brush and tell them to move towards the paper and paint what these feelings look like! You may want to set some ground rules, for example agreements not to write obscenities or other things that may be offensive.

Allow five to ten minutes and blow the whistle as a 'time up' indicator. Each young man should now stand away from where he is painting.

Stand back and review what has been created. What does it look like? Encourage the young men to ask each other about what they have painted and how 'anger' looks to them, reserving the right to 'pass' for anyone who wants it. Are there any patterns or themes emerging?

Facilitate a discussion around the experience and how it felt to use colour to represent feelings. How do they feel now? Could this be used outside the group as a way of releasing pent-up feelings? Once you have finished the discussion you can agree any further work the group would like to do around anger and conflict management.

Leave the painting on display until the end of the session.

4.9 Name that feeling!

Aim

This worksheet encourages young men to identify how they feel in different circumstances and encourages them to consider solutions that will not lead to tension and aggression.

You will need

- a copy of the '"Name that feeling!" sheet', folded into a concertina so that only the first scenario shows.

How to do it

Begin the session by talking about the wide range of emotions that we all feel. Introduce the idea that sometimes these feelings either get in the way of how we deal with a situation or are not identified correctly. So the problem remains unresolved, or becomes larger and we feel less able to deal with it. Ask the young men to think about a time when a problem got worse because of something they did or did not do. What feelings do they remember?

Hand out the '"Name that feeling!" sheet', folded up so that only the first scenario can be seen.

Ask the group to read the situation individually and consider the questions posed at the top of the sheet. If you know this will be a difficult task for your group read each scenario out to the group and ask for verbal answers.

Facilitate group feedback for each of the situations. Do the young men see the problems in the same way? Do they agree about the feelings that might arise? How easy is it to think through some ideas for solutions?

Finally encourage the group to think about some examples of their own to share and work through together.

'NAME THAT FEELING!' SHEET

For each of the situations below think about the following:

- What is the problem?

- What is the feeling?

- What can be done?

1. Your friend always has more pocket money than you do. It is not fair! Your mum is so mean – she says you should do some jobs around the house if you want more cash!

2. Your dad has left home to live with his new girlfriend. He said you could stay at weekends but now his girlfriend is saying that there is not enough room for you.

3. Someone at school is calling your brother names in the playground and threatening to break his electric wheelchair.

4. Your friend won an art competition at school. You are really fed up and think it must have been a fix. You know yours was better!

5. Your accent is different from the rest of your class. One girl keeps teasing you about this and making everyone laugh at you. When you try to answer back she just mimics you and everyone laughs more.

6. Your girlfriend dumped you by text and is now telling all her mates that you were a rubbish boyfriend.

7. You sent an email by mistake to the wrong person and now they have a picture of you when you were five years old!

8. Your stepdad threatens to ground you if you answer him back one more time.

9. You tried really hard in an exam but still didn't do well – your teacher cracks a joke about it as he hands back your paper.

10. Your new partner is at your house for the first time; you want to go to your room but your mum insists on trying to talk with you both.

4.10 Personal boundaries

Aim

This activity is intended to help participants recognise the feelings that the body sends to signal personal boundaries.

You will need

- flipchart
- markers.

How to do it

Begin by explaining that personal boundaries are made up of beliefs, opinions, attitudes and past experiences, as well as things learnt from family, faith and society.

Different people may have different boundaries, but the body signals pretty clearly when these are being threatened through our feelings. Stress to the young men that it is important to listen to these feelings and learn to trust and act upon them. In particular it is important to communicate these boundaries within personal relationships. In a positive relationship the personal boundaries of both partners should be respected and not pushed.

Now, ask the young men to call out a list of personal questions and record them on the flipchart. These should range from the general through to more intimate questions, for example:

- Do you have a girlfriend/boyfriend?
- Are you a virgin?
- Which part of your body do you like least?
- Who do you fancy and what is your secret fantasy about that person?
- What is your most embarrassing secret?

Ask the young men to choose a partner and sit facing each other. One partner should volunteer to go first and answer four questions chosen from the list and asked by their partner. Subsidiary questions are allowed and the questioner is encouraged to probe until the person being questioned raises a hand to indicate their boundaries are reached. When this happens the questioner must stop and back off.

After the four questions the partners switch roles and repeat the process.

Once both partners have asked and answered questions facilitate a feedback session. What was it like to cross a personal boundary? How did you know your boundary was being crossed? Describe the thoughts and feelings. Move on to consider how personal sexual and relationship boundaries can be explained to girlfriends/boyfriends and how to make sure that both partners are respected.

4.11 Space

Aim

This is a really good way of illustrating the concept of 'personal space'. Young men in particular are often not aware of comfort zones and this is a good way of showing them that we all have personal boundaries.

You will need

- a piece of chalk.

How to do it

Divide the group into two equal smaller groups and name them 'Group 1' and 'Group 2'.

Draw a chalk line or choose a wall to use. This activity works really well outside too. Make sure that the area is clear of potential trip hazards! Group 2 should now form a straight line along the chalk mark or wall that you have identified.

Ask Group 1 to move slowly towards Group 2, from the opposite side of the area, with their arms outstretched. Group 2 should stand as still as possible. Members of Group 2 should raise their hands in front of their chests as soon as a young person from Group 1 comes uncomfortably close to them.

Once everyone has done this and all of Group 1 has a partner from Group 2, stop. Ask everyone to stay where they are and look about. The distance or 'personal space' left between each couple will vary depending on what individuals feel comfortable with.

Reflect and discuss this with the young men. How does it feel when someone invades your personal space uninvited? What could happen if you stood this close in an argument? Could it feel threatening, for example, to young women? This can then lead on to work around keeping safe and protective behaviour as well as personal responsibilities to make others feel safe. You could suggest things such as young men giving young women space if they are walking behind them at night or crossing the road to try to make them feel more comfortable and safe. Encourage the young men to come up with their own ideas.

4.12 Express yourself

Key to emotional literacy is self-awareness and the ability to understand your own emotions and those of others. It is also important to have the skills to express these feelings effectively.

Aim

This activity encourages young men to develop their vocabulary of feelings.

You will need

- flipchart paper
- pens
- post-it notes
- 'feelings sheets' listing five key emotions.

How to do it

Before the group arrives make up 'feelings sheets' by taking five flipchart paper sheets and individually heading them 'anger', 'happiness', 'fear', 'disgust' and 'sadness'.

Divide the young men into five groups. Hand each group one of the 'feelings sheets' with a key emotion written on the top, a pen and a pack of post-it notes. Ask each group to write down as many words as they can associate with that key emotion onto individual post-it notes. For example, 'anger': irritation, annoyance, fury, rage, aggression, violence, hate.

Allow ten minutes for this process. Now ask the young men to pick up the post-it notes and rank each word according to intensity. Once they have agreed a 'feelings scale' invite each group to feedback their work. Encourage comments from the rest of the larger group – is everybody in agreement with the rankings?

Finally ask the young men to form pairs. Taking it in turns ask each young man to talk for five minutes about something important to them in their lives, past, present, or future, using as many feelings words as possible. If you think that this may not be comfortable for everyone choose positive experiences to share or reduce the time to two minutes.

4.13 Worry map

This activity works with groups of up to six people. You do need to be sensitive to personal space boundaries and refer to any group contract before you start as the activity does involve close contact.

Aim

To produce a discussion around issues that are important for the group and areas of potential stress.

You will need

- a very large sheet of paper
- an assortment of marker pens.

How to do it

Lay the sheet out on the floor in the middle of the group. Ask one of the young men to offer to lie flat on the paper and be drawn around by another member of the group. Once they have finished ask the 'template' to stand up. You should now have a life-size human silhouette to work with!

Ask the group to take a pen and in turn think of a concern or pressure that young men experience, then write it down with an arrow to where it corresponds on the silhouette body. Stress that it does not have to be an issue personal to them, but could be a worry that they think other young men may share, for example body image, lack of money or problems with parents. Encourage the group to think about all aspects of life, to include school and home. Include issues such as bullying, peer pressure and the stress of personal relationships (or lack of them!).

Agree three or four main topics that are seen as a major worry by the group and facilitate a discussion. For each topic consider things such as: is it a problem for most young men? Is it different for young women? Do they think the problems will resolve themselves, as they grow older? Are there choices or solutions that other members of the group can suggest? Who else could they talk to if this became a real problem? Close the discussion by identifying support networks, including the role of parents and friends within this.

4.14 Self-esteem – what is it?

Aim

This is an exercise to discuss the meaning of self-esteem.

You will need

- copies of the 'self-esteem cards'.

How to do it

Divide the young men into small groups of three or four. Give each group a set of the 'self-esteem cards'. Their task is to discuss each card and then rank it in terms of importance, putting the statements they think best describe self-esteem at the top, and the ones they think are least relevant and important last.

Allow about 15 minutes for discussion and then ask if each group has reached consensus. Next, facilitate a feedback session inviting the young men in each group to share their top selections and the reasons why these were chosen.

Finally, hand each young man a post-it note and pen and ask them to individually rank their own self-esteem between one and five, with one meaning low and five meaning high. Encourage group discussion about these rankings, including what increases self-esteem and what can knock it. Ask each young man to consider something he could do to develop his own self-esteem and to write down a goal on the back of the paper on which he wrote his ranking.

Make sure that these are realistic and achievable goals and then collect the papers in. Set a date for reviewing the targets set and then repeat the exercise at the end to see if there is any difference. These can then be used to show the young people's journeys and enable the young men to reflect and set new targets.

SELF-ESTEEM CARDS

Having personal goals and aspirations	Believing that I deserve love and respect	Feeling secure in myself
Being able to say what I do and don't want	Feeling worthy of my own happiness	Feeling that I can cope with life's pressures and stresses
Believing I deserve to be treated well by others	Liking myself	Feeling in control of my life and my choices

A positive belief in my own value	Taking the best possible care of myself	Knowing I have rights and responsibilities
Knowing that I can cope with changes in my life	Knowing myself and my capabilities	Feeling secure in my friendships
Believing that I have the right to express my feelings	Having the right to ask for help	Understanding that I will make mistakes

4.15 Expressing emotions

Aim

This activity builds empathy and develops young men's skills to recognise other people's emotions by their facial expressions, and to respond appropriately.

You will need

- large sheets of sugar paper
- scissors
- markers
- glue sticks
- magazines
- post-it notes
- slips of paper with one of the following emotions written on each: 'scared', 'disgusted', 'sad', 'angry', 'happy', 'surprised'.

How to do it

Divide the young men into small groups. Hand each group a piece of paper, markers, scissors, a glue stick and a selection of magazines.

Give each group a slip with an emotion written on it and ask that they don't show it to anyone yet. Explain that what you want them to do is to look through the magazines and make up a collage of faces that show the emotion on their slip. Markers can be used to enhance the collage, but not to write the actual word.

Allow about 20 minutes and then ask a representative from each group to come forward, collect Blu-Tack and display their collage on the wall. Now, view the display and hand each small group some post-it notes.

Each group should return to where they were working and agree what emotion is represented in each of the collages, including their own. These should then be stuck onto the collages. How many labels correctly identified the emotion?

Use the collages as a discussion point to consider emotions and the different ways they are expressed. Is it easy to see what other people are feeling? What happens if signs are misread? For example, you think your mum is angry with you and so react aggressively but actually she is scared of a spider she has just seen! Move on to consider if emotions are sometimes deliberately hidden and possible reasons for this, for example pretending not to care about something upsetting, again encouraging the young men to share experiences.

4.16 Stress out

Aim

This session is an introduction to managing stress and stressful situations and is a good follow-up to the previous activity. It works best with a small group of no more than six young men who have already done some work together that involves sharing feelings.

You will need

- copies of the '"Stress out!" sheet'
- red pens
- sheets of A4 paper.

How to do it

Refer to the 'worry map' that you have already completed with the group, or spend ten minutes idea-storming concerns or worries that young men may have.

Introduce the idea that different things cause stress for different people. For example, Ravi may find exams no problem, but the thought of a test makes Tom feel sick. Stress that it is normal for people to react in different ways to situations and to find different things worrying.

Give a '"Stress out!" sheet' and pen to each young man, asking them to read through the sessions and give each a stress 'rating'. Remind them that there are no wrong or right answers, just different responses. Explain that the empty box at the bottom is for them to write in their own example of a stressful situation. Once everyone has completed the task discuss the findings. Is there a top 'stress out' from the sheet? Are the answers similar or do they vary widely? Ask if anyone is willing to share a personal example and discuss this too.

Now suggest that one of the most important things about coping with stress is to recognise things that are likely to stress you out, identify what happens to your body both emotionally and physically and then develop skills and techniques to help you deal with it.

In pairs, ask the young men to choose one of the examples on the sheet, or use their own, to look at. Ask them to consider and then write down the symptoms of stress that the situation may cause, such as sweaty palms, feeling sick, aggression, etc., and then positive things that they could do to chill out and de-stress. This can include simple things such as taking deep breaths or going for a walk and more long-term solutions such as learning Tai Chi or boxing.

Ask the young men to consider what could happen if they don't use some form of stress management and the potential consequences. Once again this could range from actually being sick to getting into a fight or other aggressive behaviour.

In the large group share the findings and discuss. To close the session, as a group agree to try one of the techniques discussed to cope with a stressful situation during the next week and share the results at the next session!

'STRESS OUT!' SHEET

Have a look at the situations below and with a red pen colour in the bars to show how stressful you would find them. Colouring in one box means the situation is not stressful at all! Colouring in all six boxes means this would stress me out!

You have a row with your mum and she grounds you.	You fail an important exam you thought you'd pass.
Some lads from another school tell your mate that they are going to 'get you'.	Your girlfriend dumps you for your mate.
Your mum and dad decide to get divorced.	People at school keep talking about you.
A friend tells you she thinks she is pregnant and begs you not to tell anyone.	Your sister finds cigarettes in your room and threatens to tell your parents.
You are being bullied by someone older.	A close relative is very ill.

You move house miles away from your mates.

You are getting behind with school work.

Your pet dies suddenly.

You are being ignored by your friends.

You want to ask out someone you really fancy.

You don't want to do something that all your friends are doing.

You are caught spraying graffiti on a wall by a police officer.

You feel that you are less attractive than everyone else.

All your mates have girlfriends except you.

4.17 Stress gallery

Aim

This activity encourages young men to consider stress factors and develop some positive coping strategies.

You will need

- five large sheets of coloured paper
- a selection of coloured markers
- sticky tape
- flipchart paper.

How to do it

Ask the young men for a definition of stress. Emphasise that stress can cause powerful feelings, as well as biological changes in the body. Facilitate a short idea storm that suggests some of the feelings and biological changes that stress can cause.

Next, stick up the five large sheets of coloured paper at different points in the room. Each sheet should have one of the headings below:

- Situations that anger me
- Situations that worry me
- Situations that make me happy
- Situations that make me excited
- Situations that scare me

If you are working with a small group facilitate as a whole group activity, if not divide the main group into five smaller ones. Position each group next to one of the posters and hand out a selection of markers.

Each group has one or two minutes to write down their responses to the situation on the poster in front of them. When the designated time is up, ask each group to move to the poster on their right. Continue rotating until each group has had a chance to write their responses to the situations on all five posters.

Invite a spokesman from each group to read the responses on the poster in front of them. Discuss similarities, insights, or perceptions related to the ideas listed. Talk about which responses are positive stressors and which are negative stressors. Conclude that stress isn't necessarily a bad thing; it can be positive in some situations.

Encourage the young men to consider healthy strategies to cope with the stressful situations identified, for example, going for a walk, playing sport, using art to express feelings or talking to someone. Record these on the flipchart paper and display or type up and distribute later.

Chapter 5

Exploring Values and Attitudes

5.1 First impressions

Aim

This is a good way to start looking at stereotypes and prejudice. The point of it is that people tend to make assumptions about others based on very limited information – once you have an idea, your existing knowledge, attitudes and values complete the picture, and what you end up with is not necessarily right.

You will need

- paper and a pencil for each participant
- the aardvark description which is given below
- a picture of an aardvark.

How to do it

Hand out paper and pencils, but do not say too much about the aim of this activity. Introduce it as a quick drawing game or active listening exercise. Stress that it doesn't matter how well people can draw, this is about listening and recording information.

Once everyone has a paper and pencil ask the young men to close their eyes, and not open them again until you tell them they can! Explain that you are going to read out a description of something, and as you do you want them to listen and then draw it.

Carefully read the aardvark description allowing time for the young men to draw, but not too much time as you want them to go with their first thoughts.

Once you have finished go around the group and ask each person to show their picture and share what they thought they were drawing. In my experiences this ranges from an elephant to a rabbit! Encourage everyone to explain the mental process they went through to arrive at their decision. If anyone has guessed correctly lead a round of applause from the group.

Now show them the picture and reveal what they should have been drawing.

Reflect that often, when we are given limited information about something, we 'make up' the rest of the picture based on our experiences, knowledge, culture and values. Whilst this can be a good thing, it can also lead to false assumptions and stereotypes. Encourage the young men to reflect on a time when assumptions have been made about them that were not necessarily true. Then ask them to share experiences where they have jumped to conclusions or assumed something about somebody just because of the way they looked or talked or the music they liked.

Conclude that it is easy to assume things, but important to find out more about individuals to avoid stereotyping or judgements being made that can lead to prejudice.

The aardvark description

It has a short neck connected to a massive, dull, brownish-grey, almost hairless body. Its back is strongly arched. It has four legs. The back ones are longer than the front ones. Its head is elongated and ends in a long, narrow snout, with nostrils that can be open or closed. The ears are long and tubular shaped, normally held upright but they can be folded and closed. It has a short muscular tail that is cone shaped and tapers to a point. Finally, it has thick claws on its forefeet that are used as digging tools.

5.2 To be a man

Aim

This activity explores values and attitudes around anger and violence and then encourages young men to look at volatile situations, identify triggers and identify possible outcomes.

You will need

- photos depicting males of all ages in aggressive or angry situations
- flipchart and markers.

How to do it

Start the session by asking the young men to consider the following statement: 'To be a man you have to be able to take care of yourself.'

Facilitate a short discussion asking the young men to explain their opinions, who influences them, what they mean by 'take care' and then going on to explore some potentially volatile situations that boys/men can find themselves in.

Divide the young men into smaller groups of three or four and hand each group a picture. These could be news cuttings, for example showing football violence, or even film posters for action films. Explain to the groups that their task is to devise a role-play that explains what is happening in the picture.

Allow 20–30 minutes for the groups to practise and then invite them to take turns sharing their scenes with the whole group. Make sure that you encourage active listening during each performance and applause afterwards.

After each performance invite the audience to try and identify what made the characters angry, what the early warning signs were, how the situation escalated and what the consequences of behaviour displayed could be. Then go on to consider alternative, more positive, ways in which the situation could have been handled to avoid conflict. This should include the option of walking away.

Record these ideas on flipchart paper after each performance.

Finally, after all of the performances, facilitate a discussion that reviews the anger management techniques suggested and recorded and consider how the young men could use them in 'real life' situations.

5.3 Word bag

Aim

This is a really good way to introduce potentially controversial issues. To work effectively participants should remain anonymous so that the words written on the paper slip can be discussed freely.

You will need

- a small slip of paper for each group member
- pens
- an opaque bag.

How to do it

Set chairs in a circle and ask the young men to sit down. Give out a pen and slip of paper to each member of the group.

Tell the young men you are going to call out a word and you would like them to write on their paper what they feel when they hear the word. For example, if this is a piece of work you're developing around positive relationships you could use the word 'respect'. Explain that this can be an emotional response, a question or what they understand by the word. You will need to agree some ground rules and explain that the slips will be shared later, although they will remain anonymous. The young men's responses will enable you to explore attitudes and see what future sessions need to include.

Once the papers have been written on you can collect them in the bag, shaking it so that the papers get mixed up well. Now pass the bag back around the circle in the opposite direction. As each person takes the bag they should pull out a slip and read the contents. If they pick out their own they should fold it back up and return it for someone else.

Leave space for comments or a short discussion after each reading. Is everyone clear what the word means? Are similar issues arising? Challenge any discriminatory comments or give additional information if there is any confusion. Make sure that if identities are guessed the group does not direct their comments directly at the young man. This is a group process not an opportunity to work through issues with individuals.

You can go through the process as many times as the young men want to – encourage them to choose their own words.

Close the session by agreeing any additional work identified that the group would like to look at in the future.

5.4 Gender rules activity

Aim

To consider unwritten 'rules' relating to being male/female and the impact they have on young people.

You will need

- flipchart paper

- markers.

How to do it

Ask the young men to consider why there are rules in any society, for example to keep people safe. Are rules a good thing? What would happen if there were none? Ask the young men to suggest some of the rules that they think affect them, for example, school or home rules.

Next ask the group to consider the difference between laws, for which there is a judicial punishment if you are caught breaking them and unwritten laws that people live by. For example, it is against the law to smoke on a train, but it is an unwritten law that people do not jump a queue.

Now, divide the group up into threes or fours and hand each group a sheet of paper and a marker. They should draw a line down the middle of the sheet, and then write 'MALE' at the top of one half, and 'FEMALE' on the other. Next ask them to think about any unwritten rules that they consider to be gender specific to boys and men or girls and women, for example the unwritten rule that 'boys don't cry'.

Bring the whole group back together and ask for feedback. Encourage the young men to discuss:

- What are the unwritten rules?

- How old were they were when they received these messages?

- Who passed the message on?

- Has it affected their behaviour/attitudes/values?

Finally discuss what happens if these rules are broken.

5.5 Acceptable/unacceptable

Aim

The idea of this activity is to get the young men to think about their own values and those of their peers. If you are working with a group larger than eight split the group and use two sets of cards. Invite the young men to share and compare answers.

You will need

- a set of the 'acceptable/unacceptable situation cards'
- a card marked 'acceptable' and a card marked 'unacceptable' in a different colour from the other cards.

How to do it

Hand out the set of situation cards to the group and ask them to read each of the situations offered.

Mark two opposing poles on the floor with the 'acceptable' and 'unacceptable' cards. Explain that what you want the young men to do is to 'rate' the cards as acceptable or unacceptable behaviour. Stress that there is not always a right or wrong answer; some responses are based on cultural or social acceptance, which may differ within the group.

For each card, agreement needs to be reached within the group before it is placed in a zone. If there are different views, facilitate a discussion so that each young man's opinion is voiced. Ensure that everyone is heard and that more assertive members of the group do not try to enforce their opinions on everyone else. If no agreement can be reached for a particular card then consider a voting process.

When all the cards are placed down review the process with the young men. How easy was it to reach consensus? Was it easy to listen to views that opposed their own? How did it feel to be in the minority?

ACCEPTABLE/UNACCEPTABLE SITUATION CARDS

A man kissing a woman in the street	A young couple kissing and cuddling on a blanket in the park
An elderly couple holding hands as they walk along	A young woman slapping her boyfriend
A young man hitting his girlfriend	A young man kissing his friend's girlfriend
A man swearing at his girlfriend in public	Shouting insults down the phone at a parent
A gay couple cuddling at a party	A lesbian couple holding hands in the cinema
A young man crying	A young man telling his friends that he has had sex with his girlfriend

A woman crying	A young woman telling her friends that she has slept with her boyfriend
A couple having sex in a car after dark in a public place	A young man lying about losing his virginity
A young man hugging his male friend	Two girls kissing cheeks when they meet
Thinking a girl means 'yes' when she says 'no'	A young woman lying about who she has slept with
A woman hitting a woman	A young couple having sex at a party whilst drunk

5.6 What's in a name

Aim

This activity encourages young men to think about gender inequalities and consider any 'double standards' that exist around sexual behaviour.

You will need

- flipchart paper
- marker pens
- information about the age of consent for both heterosexual and gay/lesbian sex.

How to do it

Make a circle of chairs so that the young men can see each other. Introduce the session, being sensitive to the diversity within the group ensuring that everyone feels comfortable. Refer to the group contract and reinforce confidentiality agreements.

Ask for two volunteers to 'scribe' and seat them on either side of you with a flipchart sheet and different colour markers. Next, ask the young men to think of all the names that they have heard for a 'male'; this should include slang as well as more formal terms. For example, 'man', 'sir', 'geezer', etc. One of the volunteer scribes should write the names down with a coloured marker on the paper as they are called out.

When the group have exhausted all the names they can think of, ask the young men to think of all names for 'females'; for example 'girl', 'Mrs', 'bird', etc. Ask the other volunteer to record these on a second sheet with a different colour.

When this has been done ask the young men to look at the two lists and comment on any differences. You will find that there are usually more terms for women than men and that they often include 'baby' or pet names. Ask the group for suggestions as to why this is.

Next, repeat the exercise asking for names that describe a man who has casual sex or lots of partners and then a woman who similarly 'sleeps around'. Stress that you are not asking if individuals have ever called somebody this or believe it to be necessarily true and give permission for slang or offensive words to be included. You may want to develop this so that the young men also share who they have heard use the term. For example, 'My mum always says girls in short skirts look cheap.'

You will find that once again there are far more names and terms of abuse for women who are thought to be promiscuous than there are for men. They are also more aggressive and offensive.

Ask the young men to consider why they think this is and facilitate a discussion around the findings. Within the discussion talk about the age of consent and consider any impact, or not, this has. Do they think that acceptable sexual behaviour varies depending on which gender you are? What are their personal opinions? Ask them to reflect on their own experiences and share any examples that they can think of. Close by considering how any prejudice or inequalities could be challenged.

5.7 Jobs for the boys

Aim

This activity provokes debate as young men explore stereotypes around gender and roles.

You will need

- two A3 size sheets of paper with 'agree' on one and 'disagree' on the other

- Blu-Tack (to stick the paper to the floor).

How to do it

Set up the room in advance by sticking the 'agree' sheet on one side, and the 'disagree' on the other.

Ask the young men to listen to the following statements and then move to either the 'agree' area or the 'disagree' site. Stress that it is an individual response that you are looking for and that their first reaction is the one they should act on. If they are undecided explain that they can stay between the two areas. If they wish to change their mind at any stage they can, but encourage them to explain why.

After each movement stop to discuss issues raised. If there is disagreement, ask the 'agree' to explain to the 'disagree' what they believe. Then ask the 'disagree' group to respond. Make sure you challenge all points of view and encourage the young men to explore what informs their attitudes.

THE STATEMENTS

1.	All male hairdressers are gay.
2.	Boys are better at science than girls.
3.	It is a man's job to protect his family.
4.	Women are more emotional than men.
5.	Men are naturally better drivers than women.
6.	There are some jobs that women just can't do.
7.	Men are better chefs.
8.	Women are naturally better at caring for children.
9.	Men find it hard to have a female boss.
10.	Housework is not a man's responsibility.

5.8 Men in the news

You can use this session to review how 'men' can be shown in the media, look at assumptions made and discuss how this can impact on expectations around behaviour, both positive and negative.

Aim

The aim of this session is to promote a group discussion about a newspaper article that portrays the behaviour of boys and men.

You will need

- a selection of media stories from magazines, local and national newspapers that feature groups of adult and young men, for example stories about local gangs, drugs, football, etc.

- flipchart

- markers.

How to do it

Start the session with a group idea storm onto flipchart paper about the way 'males' are shown on TV and in the media. List all points, both positive and negative.

Then break the large group into fours and hand a copy of a news story to each smaller group. Give the young men flipchart paper and markers to write discussion points.

Allow 20 minutes for the young men to discuss the story asking them to consider the following;

- How has the media presented this story?

- What message does it give?

- Is this a fair representation?

- How does this reflect on other men?

Call the whole group back together and ask for a volunteer from each four to outline the issues on their flipchart. Are these similar regardless of the story studied? Facilitate a discussion around the findings. Are different subjects reported in different ways? Is gender an issue? How could this change? What can they do as individuals?

You can then plan follow-up sessions looking at the issues raised.

5.9 Images

Aim

The aim of this session is to raise the group's awareness of gender stereotyping in a non-confrontational way, encouraging them to open up further discussions.

You will need

- copies of the 'images word cards'
- flipchart paper
- plenty of coloured markers.

How to do it

Hand each young man a slip from the 'images word cards' and a piece of flipchart paper. Explain that each slip has on it a job or description of what a person does. Ask them to look at the word on the slip and using marker pens draw a picture of how they think that person looks. Stress that they should not tell anybody else what is on the slip at this stage. Emphasise that this is not a drawing competition and that they can use any style that they like.

Give the group ten minutes to do this and then ask them to stop and gather together with their pictures. In turn the young men should show their picture to the rest of the group who then try to guess what the person in the picture does.

When all the pictures have been correctly identified review what has been drawn. Are all the nurses shown as women? Are all the judges drawn as men? How about police and teachers? Encourage the group to discuss how they decided what gender to draw, to look at stereotypes and to consider whether they are actually representative of the profession shown.

IMAGES WORD CARDS

Police Officer	Criminal
Teacher	Head Teacher
Nurse	Doctor
Miner	Social Worker
Builder	Electrician
Parent	Hairdresser
Cleaner	Truck Driver

Judge	Car Mechanic
Pilot	Secretary
Carpenter	Retail Assistant
Lifeguard	Soldier
Chef	Model
DJ	Bar Worker

5.10 Positive relationships

Collage is a fast and fun way of creating a powerful image or message. If you have a large group divide them up so that no more than four young men are working on any one collage.

Aim

To create a collage depicting what makes a positive relationship.

You will need

- newspapers and magazines (make sure there are plenty that are aimed at the teen market)
- scissors
- glue
- markers
- large sheets of paper or card
- Blu-Tack (to stick the collages up with).

How to do it

Ask the young men, working in groups of three or four, to look through the selection of media images you have collected and produce a collage that represents 'positive relationships'. Make sure you include magazines aimed at young women that the young men may not have seen or felt comfortable in looking through before.

Hand out glue, scissors and pens. Suggest that the groups may want to add words to their images by either cutting out letters or slogans from the newspaper, or by using a marker pen.

Allow approximately 30 minutes for the young men to collate their pictures and make the collages. As they finish ask them to stick their work up and encourage the young men to look at what other groups have produced. Ask for a spokesperson from each group to explain the main points and answer any questions.

Bring the group together and use the collages as a discussion starting point. Encourage the young men to consider what images dominate the media. Are they like the people seen in real life? Are couples featured who have physical disabilities?

How are gay and lesbian relationships shown? How does it feel if you do not match the images shown? Ask the group to think where people who do not fit the stereotypes promoted can find positive role models that reflect themselves. Identify ways in which individuals can challenge inequalities.

Chapter 6

Taking Risks

6.1 Risky behaviour

Aim

This is a small group activity aiming to explore attitudes to risk-taking and promote discussion.

You will need

- flipchart paper
- markers.

How to do it

Ask the young men to choose a partner to work with and ask each pair to identify five risk-taking activities that are admired in our society. This could include things such as mountain-climbing, skiing, sailing around the world, etc.

When they have completed this task ask each pair to join another to make a four and share what they have on their lists. Facilitate a whole group feedback to discuss the types of activities identified. Are there any clear themes?

Move the discussion on to look at other forms of risk, this time looking at things that may take emotional courage rather than putting you in physical danger. For example, asking someone you fancy out, or standing up for yourself.

Now, ask the young men to go back into their fours to consider risk-taking activities that they think are not admired by society, for example playing chicken in the road or driving a car without a licence. Ask each small group to agree on five in particular and then consider common themes that run through them and any potential consequences. For example, risk-taking activities are usually unplanned, may cause harm to others, could result in a criminal, record, etc.

Whilst the young men complete their task, stick up two sheets of flipchart paper, one headed 'Admired risks', the other 'Not admired risks'. Finally, show the large group the sheets and ask for two volunteers. Hand them a coloured marker each and ask the young men to consider in turn the characteristics of admired risks and risks that are not admired. Are they the same? Discuss the differences and draw out the reasons why one set of risks are acceptable to society and the others not.

6.2 Crime sheet

This sheet is best used with small groups of young men. You will need to have built a good relationship with them so that they feel they can be honest.

Aim

To look at attitudes to crime within the group, and consider the potential consequences of offending behaviour.

You will need

- information about young people and the law
- copies of the 'crime sheet'
- pens.

How to do it

When you first introduce this sheet you will need to reassure the young men that what they share will remain confidential, unless it is a child protection issue or you are required to pass it on to the police. You will have to assess the group and their level of offending to see if this is going to be a major issue.

Reinforce that this activity is about attitude and opinions as much as fact. Also, make sure that the young men realise that you are not suggesting that you think they have done anything wrong!

If you know that the group has a short attention span or difficulties with written tasks cut the numbers of questions. Similarly you could read the questions out.

When everyone has finished go through the sheet and talk through the consequences, legally and socially, of what could happen if the examples given happened. For example, if you steal from a friend they may not report you to the police, but it would definitely damage your friendship! Encourage the young men to start to think through decisions and to consider outcomes.

Pick out any issues that the group wants to explore further and facilitate a discussion. Provide information and ask if the young men would like to focus on one or two issues to work on over the next few weeks. For example, you could offer a follow-up session that covers what happens if a young person is arrested. You could contact your local Youth Offending Team for more advice or information.

CRIME SHEET

Please look at the list below and put a tick in the box that corresponds best with what you think.

		Yes, definitely a crime	Not really a crime	No, not a crime
1.	Travelling on a bus or train without paying.			
2.	Hitting someone who calls you names.			
3.	Stealing a car.			
4.	Spraying graffiti on walls.			
5.	Carrying a knife in self-defence.			
6.	Shoplifting from a large store.			
7.	Drinking alcohol in the street.			
8.	Buying something you know is stolen.			
9.	Buying cannabis for a mate.			

10.	Giving a false name to the police.			
11.	Stealing from home.			
12.	Using someone else's password and going into their social networking account to send messages.			
13.	Going for a drive in a stolen car.			
14.	Shouting abuse at someone in the street.			
15.	Sending an abusive text message.			
16.	Damaging parked cars with a key.			
17.	Keeping money you find in the street.			
18.	Borrowing money with no intention of paying it back.			
19.	Using a parent's credit card to buy goods online.			
20.	Taking out a mobile phone contract using someone else's ID.			

6.3 Alcohol value maps

You can do this as an individual piece of work or adapt it to use as a group task. Make sure you find out in advance if there are any specific issues within the group so that you can decide if it is appropriate.

Aim

To encourage young men to consider the impact cultural and family values can have on personal attitudes to alcohol.

You will need

- A4 sheets of paper
- pens.

How to do it

Hand a sheet of paper and a pen to each young man. Explain that for the moment you would like them to work alone, although you will be inviting them to talk later. This gives them the opportunity to decide how much they want to share. Explain that the task is to draw a family tree that shows two generations of their family. If you think it is necessary draw a simple family tree on flipchart paper so that they can see what you mean.

Against the name of each family member they should write anything that they learnt or any messages given from this person about alcohol. Now indicate if this person drinks, or has ever drunk, alcohol. Now ask the young men to add friends or other members of their community to the values map with the messages about alcohol they picked up from them. Are they different?

Once they have completed this invite the young men to discuss their findings with the person sitting next to them. Encourage them to reflect on how the messages they received about alcohol impact on how they view alcohol issues now.

Feedback the main points from the different discussions into the main group pulling out any issues for further work.

6.4 Would have/should have

Aim

To consider the differences between what individuals do and what they think they should do in a range of alcohol-related circumstances.

You will need

- a copy of the 'would have/should have scenarios' sheet for each pair
- pens.

How to do it

Ask the young men if they can think of a time when they were in a difficult situation and made a decision to do something other than what they felt they should have done, for example finding money at school and not handing it in or not challenging someone bullying someone else. Conclude that sometimes we know what we should do but we do something different.

Divide the main group into smaller groups of twos or threes. Hand each group a copy of the scenarios sheets for them to discuss and make notes on. Make the point that for some scenarios what you should and would do may be the same thing. Allow 15 minutes and then bring the whole group together again.

Invite each small group to share one scenario and their agreements on what they would and should do in the circumstances. Encourage comment and invite the rest of the group to voice their opinions.

Facilitate a discussion that considers:

- Why are some of the scenarios easier to deal with than others?
- What are the possible consequences for making the 'wrong' or the 'right' decision?
- What helps in the decision-making process?

WOULD HAVE / SHOULD HAVE SCENARIOS

Scenario 1

At youth club Jamie is making good money selling cans of beer cheaply to his mates that he has stolen from his parents' shop. You have bought cans yourself from him and he always brings a good stash of cans to parties so is very popular with everyone. Tonight he sold two cans of strong lager to one of the younger girls and she has just been sick. Her parents have been called and the youth worker asks you if you know where Jamie is, which you do. What would you do?

What should you do?

Scenario 2

Joel is fed up with babysitting his younger brother Luke, who is five, whilst mum works nights. Luke loves watching TV with Joel and usually screams and cries when he is told to go to bed. This makes Joel frustrated and angry. Joel read that brandy helps people sleep and intends putting it in Luke's hot chocolate tonight so that he doesn't have to put up with the tears. Luke throws a tantrum when he is told it is bedtime as usual and Joel tells you his plans for the drink. What would you do?

What should you do?

Scenario 3

Your mum's boyfriend is a great man and you all get on well. Most nights he arrives home earlier than your mum, smelling of alcohol. He has asked you not to say anything to your mum as she doesn't like him going for a drink after work. Tonight he arrives home after your mum and is obviously very drunk, swaying and slurring his words. Your mum is so upset and you hear him promise her that he has never gone for a drink after work before and that this is a one off. What would you do?

What should you do?

Scenario 4

Zach is 13 and tells you he has added vodka to the bottle of Coke he has with him in school. He and his friend Danny drink the contents of the bottle at break and they both return to class loudly laughing and pushing each other. The teacher comes over and they start giggling when she asks what is wrong. She smells the alcohol and asks the boys if they have been drinking; Zach becomes aggressive and tells the teacher she is picking on him. What would you do?

What should you do?

6.5 The truth, the whole truth…

Aim

This session explores the sensitive issue of telling the truth and honesty to provoke discussion around the consequences of telling the truth or choosing to lie.

You will need

- a copy of the '"The truth, the whole truth…" sheet'

- pens.

How to do it

Start the session with a brief discussion about the difference between telling the truth and lying. Make sure that you are clear about the young men's understanding and be prepared to explore issues raised, for example adults not telling the truth in the past.

Hand out a copy of the sheet and a pen to each person. Consider literacy abilities and decide if you are going to support them by reading out each statement or leave them to do this alone. Once everyone has decided which boxes to tick, look through the sheet together.

Explore the consequences of each statement. For example, if they have ticked 'That's me' next to one of the statements about withholding information, ask them to consider what the positive and negative outcomes of that action might be. Similarly encourage empathy for other people's feelings in the examples given. How does their parent/carer feel if they don't come home on time and lie about where they have been? How do they feel if someone lies to them?

Close the session by thinking of three examples where it is vital to tell the truth.

'THE TRUTH, THE WHOLE TRUTH...' SHEET

Look at the statements below and consider how true they are for you. Please put a tick in the box that is most like you

	That's me	That's sometimes me	That's not me
Sometimes I tell a lie to get out of trouble.			
I don't always tell my parent/carer where I have been.			
At school I say I am ill to get out of lessons.			
I know it is important to tell the truth.			
If a police officer asked me questions I would tell her/him the truth.			
I sometimes lie about my age to get into the cinema.			
If a teacher asked about my friend I wouldn't tell on him/her.			
I often tell people I have got things that I haven't.			
If my sister asks if I like her new clothes I say 'yes' even if I don't.			
Sometimes I pretend I can't hear my mum when she tells me to do something.			
If I found £20 at school I would pretend it was mine.			
If I have done something wrong I don't own up – even if other people get into trouble.			

6.6 How safe is safe?

Aim

The aim of this session is to look at what is meant by 'safe sex' in a small, confidential and supportive group.

You will need

- small post-it notes
- pens
- two brightly coloured A4 sheets of paper
- sexual health leaflets.

How to do it

On the two coloured sheets of paper write the words 'safe' and 'less safe' and place them about two metres apart on the floor.

Give each young man a pen and three post-it notes. Ask the young men to write on their paper something a couple may do to give each other sexual pleasure. This can range from cuddling to sexual intercourse. Explain that they should do this individually and not show each other yet. Stress that you are not asking if they have done what they write down and that nobody will be questioned about their experiences.

When each young man has completed the task ask the group to take it in turn to place a paper between the 'safe' and 'less safe' poles. Once this has been done ask the group to consider if they feel all the papers are in the right place. They can then discuss with each other and agree a final sequence. For example, 'kissing' should be near the 'safe' zone whereas 'sex without a condom' will be close to the 'less safe' area.

Once an agreement has been reached facilitate a discussion around how some 'less safe' activities can be made more 'safe' and the importance in preventing unwanted pregnancies and sexually transmitted infections. This can be supported with relevant leaflets. Discuss the findings in the context of positive relationships and keeping healthy.

6.7 Sexual health myth or fact?

This tests out some well-known assumptions about sex and pregnancy and asks young men to decide if they are 'myth' or 'fact'. You may need to get parental consent for some young people to take part in this session.

Aim

This activity will give you a good understanding of the knowledge within the group and their attitudes to sex and relationships.

You will need

- the list of 'myth or fact?' statements

- a 'myth' card and a 'fact' card for each young person taking part

- appropriate leaflets and contact numbers for your local family planning and sexual health clinic.

How to do it

Before the young men arrive prepare for the session by setting up a circle of chairs. Make up two cards for each person using green and red card. Write 'myth' on all the red cards and 'fact' on the green ones.

Seat the young men in a circle and hand out a red and green card to each participant explaining what they mean. Explain that you are going to read out a series of statements and the task is for the young men to decide if they are a 'myth' or a 'fact'. After each statement everyone should raise the card that they think corresponds with the answer. Make sure that you point out that it does not matter if people do not know all the answers and that you are not asking about personal experiences.

Be prepared to answer questions and discuss each point as it is raised. Encourage discussion and ask the group to think of other myths around sex and contraception.

MYTH OR FACT?

1. If you do it standing up you don't need contraception.

Myth – if you have unprotected sex you are at risk of the female becoming pregnant however you do it!

2. If you have sex when your partner has her period she can't get pregnant.

Myth – ovulation can happen at the same time as a period so she could get pregnant.

3. If she goes to the toilet straight after sex she won't get pregnant.

Myth – only recognised methods of contraception protect against unwanted pregnancy. Sperm travels quickly inside the vagina to the womb so the time to take precautions is before intercourse.

4. If you pull out before you come you don't need a condom.

Myth – you do need a condom if you don't want to run the risk of unplanned pregnancy! Sperm can leak out of the penis before a man comes so take care to always put on a condom.

5. You can get free condoms at the family planning clinic.
Fact.

6. Condoms are a good way to protect against sexually transmitted infections.

Fact – condoms are the best protection from STIs.

7. If you use two condoms at once it is safer.

Myth – it actually makes them less effective! Condoms used properly are an effective form of contraception. You can get extra-strong condoms for anal sex.

8. You can make a man ill if he has an erection and doesn't come.

Myth – a man does not have to ejaculate every time he has an erection.

9. It is a good idea to use baby oil with condoms.

Myth – it is a very bad idea! The baby oil (and any other oil-based product) can damage the condom and cause it to split. You can buy specially formulated lubricant at most chemists.

10. The emergency or 'morning after' pill only works the next morning.

Myth – although often called the morning after pill it can actually work up to 72 hours after sex.

11. Only a doctor can tell someone if they are pregnant.

Myth – shop-bought pregnancy kits are very effective. However, if you think your sexual partner may be pregnant encourage her to consult a doctor.

12. If you masturbate too often it can harm you.

Myth – masturbation is part of being a normal, healthy person.

13. No one gets pregnant the first time they do it.

Myth – once a girl starts having periods she can get pregnant if you have penetrative sex.

14. Some girls say 'no' when they mean 'yes'.

Myth – sex must always be consensual. If someone says 'no' and you go ahead anyway it is rape.

6.8 What happened next?

This activity encourages young men to think through difficult situations and the potential gains or losses of being assertive, telling the truth and resolving problems. Add an additional scenario that represents an issue or problem for your group.

Aim

To develop assertiveness in expressing feelings, emphasise the right to say 'no' and build awareness of the potential consequences of actions.

You will need

- the '"What happened next?" scenarios' sheet
- a storyboard sheet for each young man
- pens.

How to do it

Photocopy the scenarios sheet and cut it into slips to hand out to the young men you are working with. It doesn't matter if more than one person has the same scenario to work from. If reading is an issue, use fewer scenarios and read them out to the group.

Explain that the idea of the activity is to develop a storyboard that works through the situation on their slip looking at potential ways of handling the situation and the possible consequences.

Then, break the large group into two. Set one half the task of showing what might happen if they tell the truth about how they feel and do what they would like to. The other half should look at what could happen if they decided to lie or go along with something they are not happy with. They can do this either as themselves, thinking about their own family, friends, etc. or through the character to de-personalise it. Either way, encourage the group to reflect on their own experiences of what happens when you are faced with a difficult decision. Stress that cartoons or stick people are fine!

Hand out a copy of the storyboard sheet and make a good selection of pens available. Allow between 10 and 15 minutes for the storyboards to be completed. Now ask the young men to discuss their storyboards in pairs. Invite them to share what they have drawn, discussing how they handled the situation and why.

Bring the young men all together again and facilitate a whole group discussion, based on the conversations that the young men have had in their pairs. Which was the easier option – to say how you feel or go along with the crowd? How easy is it to say 'no' to friends? What about when it is something you really want to say 'yes' to, for example, the young man who didn't want to stay in babysitting? Discuss the potential gains and losses for doing the 'right' thing. Move on to look at what could happen if they did go along with something they are uncomfortable with, for example, stealing alcohol from home. Any issues highlighted can be used to plan further sessions.

'WHAT HAPPENED NEXT?' SCENARIOS

Your best mate has started truanting from school. He wants you to go with him – it is easy, just to go in for registration and then leave out the back. You are really tempted, but what if you get caught?

Your dad asks you to babysit for your little stepbrother – again. You are sick of it and invite a mate round to watch TV with. It is really boring and your mate wants to go to the shops where everyone else is for a bit. You really want to go too – your brother is fast asleep and you are sure it will be all right…

Some of the lads that you hang around with have started smoking the odd bit of puff. You are not really keen on the idea but you don't want to look a fool if you refuse. What are you going to do?

After Saturday's party a group of lads at school are talking about the girls they met and sex. You begin to feel panicky – it seems that they are all more experienced than you and it is your turn next…

You are invited to your mate's house whilst his foster-parents are out for a party. The evening has been a right laugh but now someone has accidentally broken the DVD player and your friend is worried sick that he will be in real trouble. You know it was you…

A girl that you really fancy asks you if you are going to the park this evening. You say 'yes', but now it has all gone wrong because she wants you to nick some alcohol from home to bring with you and you don't want to…

STORYBOARD: WHAT HAPPENED NEXT?

Use the storyboard to show what you decide to do.

6.9 Personal safety

Aim

This session introduces young men to the idea that there are things they can do to enable them to keep safe. You could open the session with a discussion about a newspaper article that reports an assault or mugging of a young man and reinforce the fact that young men can be victims of crime. The session also provides a framework for keeping safe and looks at ways to be assertive in situations in which the young men may not feel comfortable.

You will need

- a copy of the 'personal safety sheet', enlarged and cut up
- two sheets of coloured paper, marked 'OK' and 'not OK'.

How to do it

Place the sheet marked 'OK' and the other sheet marked 'not OK' on the ground about two metres apart.

Hand out the cut-up 'personal safety sheet'. Ask the young men to place them between the two sheets of paper where they feel that they should be positioned. Explain that the 'OK' zone is for situations where they feel most comfortable and confident, and the 'not OK' zone is for situations that they find unacceptable or would find worrying. Any they are not sure of should go in the middle. If there is any disagreement, facilitate comments and discussion.

For those examples that the group find unacceptable, ask the group to discuss why they are not OK, what the risks are and what could happen. Then ask the young men to suggest ways in which they could make the situation safer and how they could be assertive, and look at potential resolutions.

For any situations in the middle encourage discussion until the group can agree.

PERSONAL SAFETY SHEET

You miss the last night bus back from town and have to walk home alone.
Your mum's friend asks you for a kiss at a family party.
You have fireworks that you plan to let off with your friends.
A mate dares you to walk across a high bridge over the railway.
You are in a public toilet and a stranger approaches you and starts talking.
Your ex-girlfriend has lied to all her mates saying that you hit her.

A mate of yours offers you a lift home – you know that he has been smoking cannabis.

A younger boy at school has been caught smoking – he told the teacher that you gave the cigarettes to him.

All your mates are up for a fight with another group and expect you to go too.

Everyone wants you to go into the off-licence and try to buy some beers as you look the oldest .

6.10 Follow the crowd

Aim

This exercise asks young men to consider the consequences of their actions in potential situations. You can alter the situations to fit with issues relevant to the group you are working with.

You will need

- copies of the 'follow the crowd sheet'
- pens.

How to do it

Ask the young men to consider a time when they have 'followed the crowd' and done something that they knew was not right, but did it because friends did. Explain that they do not have to share this unless they really want to, but to think about the choices they had and what made the decision for them.

Hand out a 'follow the crowd sheet' and a pen to each participant and ask them to look at each situation and consider what the 'plus' and 'minus' points for following the crowd might be. For example, if a group of young people write their names on the wall and you decide to join in, the 'plus' might be that you become accepted as part of their gang. The 'minus' point may be that a neighbour sees it, recognises you and tells your parents.

When everyone has completed their sheet, encourage discussion about the potential 'plus' and 'minus' points for each scenario. Conclude by facilitating a discussion that looks at ways in which young men in similar difficult situations could be assertive and say 'no' without losing face within the peer group.

FOLLOW THE CROWD SHEET

Think about the 'plus' and 'minus' points about joining in with the following situations.

1. Joining in with a group that are bullying another pupil at school.

PLUS ………………………………………………………………………

MINUS ……………………………………………………………………

2. Joining in with a group that are being unkind to a stray cat.

PLUS ………………………………………………………………………

MINUS ……………………………………………………………………

3. Joining in with a group who are using stolen credit cards to make online purchases.

PLUS ………………………………………………………………………

MINUS ……………………………………………………………………

4. Joining in with a friend who is lying to his parents to get out of trouble.

PLUS ………………………………………………………………………

MINUS ……………………………………………………………………

5. Joining in with a group that stay out late drinking alcohol in the park.

PLUS ………………………………………………………………………

MINUS ……………………………………………………………………

6. Joining in with a friend who is threatening to assault someone else.

PLUS ………………………………………………………………………

MINUS ……………………………………………………………………

Chapter 7

Working Together

7.1 Fill the bottle

Aim

This is an outdoor team game that encourages the young men to work together to achieve a group task.

You will need

- a large empty plastic bottle, a bucket and a sponge for each team
- chalk.

How to do it

Divide the main group into smaller teams, with a minimum of five young men in each. Make sure that you warn everyone that they are likely to get wet taking part!

Designate a game area; you need a width of about eight metres. Ask each team to line up on one side of the game area and place an empty bottle on the opposite side. Using chalk draw a 'start' line in front of the teams and put a bucket of water on the start line.

Hand the first player in each team a sponge. They should dip this into the bucket and run across the room to the bottle, squeeze the water from the sponge into the bottle and then run back. The sponge is then passed to the next member of the team and the first player joins the back of the line.

The team that fills the bottle with most water wins.

7.2 Pass the peanut

If you are working with a really big group, just increase the peanut to young men ratio!

Aim

This game requires co-operation more than skill. It also encourages positive touch as to achieve the task and win the game the young men must hold hands. Do a quick risk assessment and make sure that no one in the group has a peanut allergy before you start.

You will need

- four dishes
- 20 peanuts.

How to do it

Divide the young men into two equal teams and ask them to line up, holding hands.

Put a dish with ten peanuts at one end of each line and an empty dish at the other end of the line.

The first person in each line picks up a peanut with his free hand and then passes it to his other hand, without letting go of his team-mate's hand. The next in line then passes the peanut from one hand to the other (which is clasped to the person on his other side) and so on, until the peanut gets to the last person, who drops it in the empty dish with his free hand. If anyone lets go of his team-mate's hand at any time, the peanut has to go back to the young man at the front of the line to start again.

The winner is the team that passes all ten peanuts into the empty dish first without unclasping their hands at any time during the game!

7.3 Rip it up!

Aim

This is a quick warm-up game to re-energise a group after discussion work.

You will need

- sheets of newspaper
- prizes (optional).

How to do it

Ask the young men to stand in a circle with their hands behind their backs, instructing them to keep their hands there for the duration of the game. Now, walk around the outside of the circle placing a sheet of newspaper in each player's hands. On the shout 'Go!' they should set to ripping the paper into the shape of whatever letter you call out – still with their hands behind their back. As they complete the task the young men should hold up the letter they have ripped above their heads. Last person to finish is out. Anyone with a totally unrecognisable letter is disqualified.

Keep going until you have two young men left competing. Either carry on with a new letter for the final round, or if you want to make the challenge harder, call out a short word for them to rip! The winner gets the respect of his peers and a loud round of applause – prizes are optional!

7.4 Blindfold trust game

Aim

The aim of this task is for members of the group to experience being the 'trusted' and the 'trusting'. It encourages them to consider how their own actions impact on others and how that feels in reverse.

You will need

- a scarf to use as a blindfold
- an obstacle course
- a watch.

How to do it

In preparation for the session identify an area to work in and set up an obstacle course for the young men to navigate. It is a good idea to do a risk assessment before the session to check that the area is safe and is not full of potential trip hazards. The same applies if you decide to play the game outside.

Ask for a volunteer. Explain to them that the point of this activity is to encourage trust in each other and that it is an opportunity to take responsibility for their own and others' safety. Tell the boys that if they feel really uncomfortable at any point in the exercise they should say, and the group will stop.

Ask the volunteer to step forward and blindfold them. Make sure that they cannot see anything and ask them to describe how that feels. Lead the young man, with his eyes still covered, to the area that you have set up.

Choose another member of the group to direct the volunteer around the obstacles. Explain that it is their job to make sure that the young man who is blindfolded gets around the area from start to finish. They must do this by giving instructions that steer him safely around the objects that you have set up and back to the start point. This will be timed – the pair with the fastest time wins the game!

During each attempt no one else in the group is allowed to help in any way. Explain that their role is to support the young man who has the blindfold on by keeping quiet so that he can hear the instructions the young man directing will give. As each young man negotiates the course blindfold ask him to reflect on his feelings, particularly if the person leading loses concentration or is careless in his directions.

Take it in turns until each person has had a go at directing and being blindfolded and directed.

Total up the times and decide the pair with the fastest time; they are the winners!

When the game is finished ask the young men for feedback. How did it feel to be dependent on someone? Was it better to be directed or the director? Did it make a difference if you chose your partner? How did it feel if they gave you bad information?

Conclude by agreeing principles for trust and look at how this fits with any friendship work that you have been doing.

7.5 Don't fall in

Aim

This is a team-building exercise that can be played indoors or outside. The more young men in the group the more effort is needed to complete the task. However, I think that it would not be much fun with less than six young men.

You will need

- No equipment is needed, but you will need to have identified an area suitable for the game. You could use a kerbstone, if it is safe, or a railway sleeper, a low breakwater or apparatus in a park. If you are inside, consider long benches or forms. For safety reasons I would be careful about using anything too high. If you can find nowhere then use chalk to draw a thick line to use.

How to do it

Ask the young men to stand side by side in a row along your designated area.

Once they have taken up position along the line, stop and tell everyone to stay still. Now, explain to the group that the object of the task you are setting is to arrange themselves along the kerb in order of their month of birth as fast as possible. Show the young men the end which is 'January' and which is 'December'.

Set a maximum time to complete this according to the size of the group – the larger the group the more time needed!

There are rules to this:

1. The order is according to the month they were born.

2. Once the young men are in a line along the straight area, no one must touch the ground on either side throughout the task. You can embellish this as much as you like depending on the age of the group and how well you know them. For example, the area on either side can become crocodile-infested water or quicksand!

3. The whole group has to decide and agree a position before any person can move.

4. The young men can enable each other to move about to get into order, for example holding hands or helping a friend balance.

5. The youth workers are there to facilitate, not to advise, but can intervene if any suggestion is dangerous.

Once the task has been completed, review it. How easy was it? What roles did people take? How did it feel when they were successful?

7.6 Pass the sound

This game can be played with young men of any age, but you do really need a group of six or more to make it work. You can impose time limits or widen the circle to make the task harder! Whichever way you decide to play, keep the pace fast!

Aim

To pass the object without making a sound!

You will need

- a bunch of keys, a bell or a musical instrument such as a tambourine.

How to do it

Ask the young men to sit on the floor in a circle, facing into the centre. Join the group and show the young men the keys or instrument you have chosen. Tambourines or bells are really good for this game!

Explain that the task is for each person in the group to pass the instrument to the person sitting on their left without making a noise! Anyone making a noise is 'out' and should leave the circle. This is lot harder than it sounds so you may want to have a practice run before you start the game! The last person in the circle wins the game and facilitates the next part of the session.

7.7 The sun shines on...

This is a good, fast game to use between activities or when you think that the young men need a break. The larger the group the more space you will need for them to run around!

Aim

The main idea of the game is to identify commonalities within the group. You can also use it as an introduction to a specific issue by setting a theme.

You will need

- chairs.

How you do it

Set up a circle of chairs, with one chair less than the number of people in the group. Don't forget to include a chair for yourself! The facilitator should then start the game by standing in the middle of the circle and asking the young men to each take a seat. These then become 'safe' spots.

The person in the middle then calls out, 'The sun shines on everyone who/ with...' They complete the sentence with something true for them as well as potentially true for other members of the group.

Everyone that this includes then runs across the circle as fast as they can to a safe spot and sits down. The only rule is that no one can move to the seat next to the one they are sitting on (unless they are the only two players in that round). The person who does not get to a safe spot then goes into the middle and the process starts again.

Ideas

- everyone with blue eyes
- everyone with a tattoo
- everyone who has a sister
- everyone who plays football.

Make sure that everyone in the group is included. Also don't call out things you are not prepared to explain – for example where your tattoo is!

The game goes on for as long as the young men want it to!

7.8 Jigsaw trial

Aim

This is a team problem-solving exercise that works well with large groups.

You will need

- large jigsaw puzzle
- envelopes.

How to do it

To prepare for the session divide a large jigsaw (110 pieces plus) into five piles, and then place the piles inside five envelopes. If you have a small number of young men adapt the activity by using a smaller puzzle and dividing it into fewer envelopes. The idea is that each envelope should look as though it contains a separate puzzle.

Divide the young men into five teams and allocate each team an area to work in – preferably where groups cannot see each other. Give each team an envelope and instruct them to assemble the puzzle inside it as quickly as possible. Say, 'The task of each team is to assemble the puzzle as quickly as possible. Each team has the same puzzle. No further instructions will be given.' The aim is for the young men to solve the problem without the aid of the facilitator.

The young men tend to assume they are competing against each other, but of course there is only one jigsaw puzzle. They usually work it out and eventually understand that the pieces to the puzzle are distributed around the teams. The only way to do the puzzle is to work together, negotiating for pieces.

Facilitate the rest of the session so that the teams work out a way to complete the puzzle and make it whole. When the task is complete reflect on the roles that individuals took during the process. Was anyone a clear leader? Did any of the young men make things easier or harder?

7.9 Peg it!

You can play this version of tag with any size of group. If you have more than 12 young men playing you may want to have two 'peg its'.

Aim

To keep hold of as many pegs as possible by evading the 'peg it'!

You will need

- three pegs per player
- two pegs for the 'peg it'.

How to do it

Choose a young man to be the 'peg it' to start the game and hand him two pegs. These need to be clipped to his collar or the neck of his T-shirt. Hand out three pegs each to the remainder of the group. They should help each other to clip their pegs along the back bottom hem of their top.

Explain that when you clap your hands the game begins. The 'peg it' will chase the rest of the young men trying his best to whip a peg off from the back of their shirts. If he manages to capture one he then clips it with the other two on his collar.

When the 'peg it' has captured all three pegs from someone, they then turn into a 'peg it' too and the game continues. As the game progresses the number of 'peg its' increases, making it more difficult to escape. The game ends when only one person with pegs on his back remains. That person is the winner!

Chapter 8

Endings

8.1 Evaluation tree

This is a creative way of evaluating a session, asking the minimum of each young man to create a visual representation of the group experience.

Aim

To build a 'tree' that describes the learning that has taken place in the session.

You will need

- a large piece of paper with a basic drawing of a tree with no leaves on it
- Blu-Tack
- pieces of paper shaped like leaves
- pens.

How to do it

Using the Blu-Tack stick your picture onto a wall and introduce it as an evaluation tree. Hand out a leaf, a pen and a small piece of Blu-Tack to each group member. Ask them to think carefully and write on the leaf a comment that describes what they have learnt during the session. You can change what you ask for to correspond with what you are trying to evaluate; for example which activity did the young men enjoy most? Or 'what did they learn from the role play?'

When they have written something ask each young man to stick his leaf onto the evaluation tree. Review the completed tree with the group and reflect on what has been written. You can then keep the tree as recorded evidence of learning.

8.2 Personal assessment

This evaluation sheet asks for a very personal view of the session in which the young men have just participated.

Aim

To encourage the young men to acknowledge the part other members of the group have played in their learning, as well as their own achievements.

You will need

- copies of the 'my personal assessment' sheet
- pens.

How to do it

Hand out copies of the sheet and ask the young men to look and think about the statements it contains. Ask them to reflect on the session they have just experienced and fill in the gaps. Depending on how well you know the group and the level of confidence the young men have, encourage the group to share their responses. If you do not think that this would be appropriate you can discuss them individually or collect them in and review later.

MY PERSONAL ASSESSMENT

My name . . . .

Date . . . .

I am pleased . . . . is here because . . . .

. . . .

. . . .

I would like to thank . . . . because . . . .

. . . .

. . . .

I enjoyed doing . . . . because . . . .

. . . .

. . . .

I learnt . . . . about myself and . . . .

. . . . about others

Things I would like to do again: . . . .

. . . .

Things I would like to do differently: . . . .

. . . .

I would like to meet with the group again because . . . .

. . . .

. . . .

My thought for next time is . . . .

. . . .

. . . .

8.3 Chain reaction

Aim

This builds on work around self-esteem and confidence, encouraging the group to reflect on their experiences and share things they are good at, whilst appreciating the talents of others.

You will need

- packets of paper chains
- marker pens.

How to do it

Begin by asking the young men, 'What skills do you think that you have?' Stress that this doesn't have to be an academic achievement but can be anything. Encourage them to reflect on the session they have just done and identify things that they contributed to the group. This can be practical, for example taking the leadership role in the team or using their artistic skills to draw the storyboard. Alternatively it could be their personal skills that have been used, for example offering someone else emotional support. After a brief discussion, conclude that everyone is talented in some way.

Now, hand out five of the unmade paper chains to each member of the group. Using markers, ask everyone to write one talent on each strip of paper. Demonstrate how to create a paper chain with their strips linking their five talents together. As the young men begin to complete their mini chains, use extra strips of paper to link the mini chains together to create one long group chain. Invite the young men to stand and hold the ever-growing chain as you link it together, until everyone is linked.

Once the entire chain is constructed and linked together, hang the chain up in the room as a reminder that everyone is skilled, talented and good at something. Encourage the young men to look at the different talents and skills within the group and refer to these during future group sessions.

8.4 Appreciation web

This visual form of evaluation is more to do with finding out how the group feels about each other and the relationship dynamics, rather than the activity. It works well with all ages, but for the best results you need the space to sit down and spread out a bit.

Aim

To enable the young men to reflect on the relationships they have with each other and the youth workers and evaluate the effectiveness of the group work.

You will need

- a ball of string or wool.

How to do it

Make a large circle, including the facilitators within the group.

Start the process yourself to demonstrate. Keeping hold of one end, throw the ball of coloured string to another member of the group saying 'The thing I appreciate about you is…' and following it up with a comment that reflects their contribution to the group. For example, this could be something like 'the way you helped me earlier' or something more personal such as 'your sense of humour'. You may want to make some ground rules about this with the young men before you start so it doesn't get too personal or make people feel uncomfortable.

As the exercise progresses you will begin to see a web forming. This is a visualisation of the process. Be really sensitive here to anyone who looks like they are feeling excluded and throw the string to them when it is your turn to contribute again.

Finally, ask the young men to put the string 'web' down in front of them onto the ground and step away. From this you can all see the interaction of the whole group.

8.5 Positive steps

Aim

This review of learning encourages the young men to think about something that they have learnt through the time spent in the group and to identify something positive that they will do for the future. You can do this either individually or as a whole group.

You will need

*   nothing.

How to do it

Ask the young men to sit down in a wide circle. Explain that what you would like them to do is to say 'goodbye' to the group and identify one positive 'step' that they are going to make as a direct result of the work that they have done in the session. So for example, 'Goodbye, I am going to try hard to be more assertive next time I am asked my opinion' or, 'Goodbye, I will ask for help in class if I do not understand rather than shout at my teacher.'

Finally, go around the circle again and ask the young men to close the session by saying one positive thing about the group itself. Close by adding a comment about what you have learnt from the group experience.

8.6 Treasured comments

Aim

The aim of this review is for young people to experience giving and receiving positive comments by creating 'treasure boxes'.

You will need

- an envelope per person with a copy of a 'treasure chest' picture stuck onto it
- coloured paper cut into strips to fit into the envelopes
- pens.

How to do it

Give each member of the group a 'treasure chest' envelope and ask them to write their name on it. Explain that this treasure chest will contain all sorts of positive messages to them by the end of the activity.

Next, provide each young man with enough brightly coloured paper strips to write a message to each member of the group. Encourage everyone to spend time thinking of something positive to say about each other. They should then write that positive message on one of the coloured strips.

When everyone has finished writing their comments, they should walk around and put their messages in one another's envelopes. At the end of the activity, each young man will have a 'treasured comments chest' to read on their own.

8.7 Evaluation shields

This is a whole group evaluation, but it works equally well with individual young men. It is a good way of encouraging those with poor literacy skills to take part as you can decide to make it entirely pictorial.

Aim

The aim is to create a piece of art that reflects the group experience and learning outcomes.

You will need

- flipchart paper
- lots of coloured markers and pens.

How to do it

Give the young men a sheet of paper and ask them to choose some pens to work with. If you have a large group divide the young people into fours so that everyone gets an opportunity to participate.

Ask the group to draw a large shield shape in the middle of the paper. Explain that this is not a test of how well they draw and they do not have to produce the same shaped shield. Once this is done the shield should be divided into three equal areas.

Explain that each third will represent the group and different things that they have been working on. The first is 'expectations' and should show what they wanted to get out of the group or what they thought it would be like. The second is the 'learning zone', representing individual and group learning, and the third is 'goals' for the future or what they plan to do now as a result of the work they have done. The depth of the information on the shields will vary depending on how well you know the young men, but it is always good to draw up some kind of agreement around confidentiality before you start.

Pass the shield around the group so that every member can write or draw in each of the sections. Finally ask the young men to add a 'motto' underneath that represents the group. For example, 'Mars Young Men's Group – helps us work, rest and play!' When everyone has completed their shield bring the group back together and form a circle. Each group can then share ideas.

8.8 Evaluation questionnaire

Aim

This is a more traditional form of evaluation that encourages the young men to reflect on their experiences. It is also a really good way of assessing how successful an activity has been with a group.

You will need

- copies of the 'evaluation questionnaire'
- pens.

How to do it

Hand out copies of the questionnaire and a pen to each participant. Ask the young men to consider the activity that they have just taken part in, their role and what learning has taken place and then answer the questions on the sheet. Encourage the young men to share their responses as they record them and discuss the session together.

Collect the sheets in and review them. The comments made will inform any follow-up work or how you structure the session if you plan to run it again with another group.

EVALUATION QUESTIONNAIRE

Name	Date

Please have a look at the questions below and answer as fully as you can.

1. What was the most interesting part of the session you have just taken part in?	2. What part was the least interesting to you?
3. Was the information relevant/useful to you?	4. Have you taken part in similar sessions before? What and where?

5. Did you enjoy it? Why?	6. What other areas did you expect to be covered?
7. What did you learn?	8. How could you have learnt more?

9. Give this session marks out of 10

8.9 Action planning

Aim

This action-planning sheet enables young men to set themselves personal goals, to be reviewed in future sessions.

You will need

- copies of the 'action planning sheet'
- pens.

How to do it

As a whole group review the session you have just facilitated. Then hand out copies of the 'action planning sheet' and a pen to each member of the group.

Encourage the young men to set themselves three realistic and achievable goals and agree a timescale to do them in. This could be something like 'I am going to walk to school for three weeks', or could be about changing a behaviour, for example 'I am going to walk away next time I get into an argument rather than fighting.' Ask the young men to sign their sheets and counter sign them yourself, writing the date of the pledge in the area provided.

Take copies of the sheets and give one to the young man and keep one to remind and support them towards meeting their goals. Review them at a future pre-arranged session.

ACTION PLANNING SHEET

NAME	
WHAT DO I WANT TO ACHIEVE?	
WHAT STOPS ME?	
WHAT HELPS ME?	

HERE ARE MY GOALS	
	1.
	2.
	3.

BY WHEN?	
REVIEW AND UPDATE	Date
	Date

Signed ....

Signed ....

Date ....

8.10 Evaluation wall

This provides ongoing feedback of how young men perceive the group work programme you are facilitating. You can leave it up for set blocks of time before updating it so that the information and comments remain relevant and 'owned' by the young men.

Aim

To encourage ownership of the evaluation process by the group and to make a record of what they are learning.

You will need

- markers
- a large printed name tag
- rolls of coloured paper
- string
- drawing pins.

How to do it

Identify a large area of wall or notice board that you can use as your evaluation wall. Cover the area in coloured paper and attach several markers to the edges using the string and drawing pins. If you are working in a school or careers centre where the room will have other users between group meetings, you can still use the same idea. Adapt the 'wall' onto a roll of paper that can be taken down after each meeting and put up again at the start of the next.

Print off a large tag with the group's name on it and put it in place at the top of the evaluation wall.

Introduce the area to the young men during the next session. Explain that this is their area to write up comments and ideas. You may want to agree ground rules with the group about appropriate language, etc., but make sure you stress that it is up to them what they choose to put there.

You will need to agree how often you are going to update the wall, as information goes out of date quickly and you want the young men to feel an ownership of the process. Inform the group when you intend to change the paper and what you are going to do with the contents.

8.11 Video diary

This method of evaluation owes much to the success of TV programmes like Big Brother and will need little explanation! It is fast, fun and encourages the young men to be honest.

Aim

To allow each young man space to 'talk' to the camera about the activity or session in which they have just taken part.

You will need

- a video camera

- tripod stand for the video camera

- parental consent to use the film or any pictures (where required).

How to do it

Set up a video 'booth' where the young men can sit quietly away from the rest of the group. All you need is a chair facing the camera on the tripod. It looks better for the replay if you have a blank wall behind the chair or a piece of cloth as a backdrop.

Introduce the evaluation process and explain that at some point during the last session Big Brother is going to call each of them into the video booth to ask for their evaluation of the group. Make sure you tell the young men who is going to see the video footage and what you are going to use it for. Also stress that no Big Brother evictions are going to be made!

If you want to play the video back to the whole group at a later stage, you will need to get agreement from everyone. They need to be clear what is happening so that they can choose what to say! Additionally you may need to get parent/carer consent if you plan to show the film to a wider audience.

Invite each young man in turn, by calling out his name, to enter the booth and speak privately to the camera. This should encourage them to be honest in their responses. This is also a good evaluation method for groups that include young men who are not comfortable reading or writing.

Finally, add your co-workers' and your own comments to the film so that you have a complete recording of everyone's account of how the group went!

Useful Websites

These websites contain information about topics relating to young men and can be useful for updating legislation and knowledge. However, the author can take no responsibility for the contents and the views expressed are not necessarily shared or endorsed because they are included.

UK websites

www.avert.org
AVERT is an international HIV and AIDS charity with specific resources for young men.

www.bullying.co.uk
Bullying UK is a website that offers support and advice to the victims of bullying and their families.

www.childline.org.uk
ChildLine is a charity offering information and support.

www.drugscope.org.uk
Drugscope is a UK charity providing up-to-date information on drug issues.

www.likeitis.org.uk
Likeitis gives young people information and advice on sexual health.

www.need2know.co.uk/health
The need2know UK website offers information, advice and support to young people on a range of issues, including relationships, health and student life.

www.nya.org.uk

The National Youth Agency works in partnership with a wide range of public, private and voluntary sector organisations in the UK to support and improve services for young people.

www.rd4u.org.uk

The RD4U website offers support to bereaved young people and includes a 'Lads Only' section.

www.survivorsuk.org

Survivors UK offers help and information for young men who have been sexually abused or raped.

www.talktofrank.com

The FRANK website offers drugs information and support.

www.thecalmzone.net

The Campaign Against Living Miserably (CALM) is targeted at young men aged 15–35. It offers help, inofrmation and advice about depression via a phone and web service.

www.ukyouth.org

UK Youth is the leading national youth work charity helping young people to realise their potential and have their achievements recognised via non-formal, accredited education programmes and activities.

www.yjb.gov.uk

The Youth Justice Board provides information and updates on the laws and orders relating to young people.

US and Australian websites

www.australia.gov.au/people/youth

The Australian government website has a youth section that offers information and links to other youth organisations.

www.hiphop4lifeonline.com

Hip Hop 4 Life is a US champion of positive youth development and empowerment, serving young people of ages 12 to 18, with a special emphasis on those residing in at-risk environments. It includes Man Up! An Empowerment Program For Boys (ages 10 to 17).

www.youthbeyondblue.com

Youthbeyondblue is an Australian website that offers support, advice and information to young people suffering stress or depression.

www.youth.gov.au/ayf/

The Australian Youth Forum (AYF) is run by the Australian government as a communication channel between the government, young people (aged 15 to 24) and the organisations that work with, for and on behalf of young people.

www.youthrights.org

The National Youth Rights Association (NYRA) defends the civil and human rights of young people in the United States through educating people about youth rights, empowering young people to work on their own behalf in defence of their rights.

Working with Young Women
Activities for Exploring Personal, Social and Emotional Issues

Vanessa Rogers

ISBN 9781849050951
Paperback: £17.99/$29.95

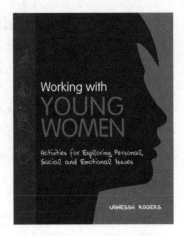

Packed with fun and imaginative games and activities, from the 'name game' to quizzes, life story games and art activities, this practical book offers a wealth of ways to engage with young women in a variety of settings.

Work with Young Women presents a multitude of opportunities to build self-esteem, confidence and assertiveness, as well as learn new skills. Issues covered include body image, positive relationships and peer choices, work around alcohol and healthy lifestyles, and gender and stereotyping. Activities, games, discussions, art and role-play are all used in working to achieve these goals. The author also discusses how to set up group work, how to get started, and how to end on a positive note. The activities are appropriate for all young women, and include suggestions for those who have special educational needs and adaptations for one-to-one work.

This second edition has been updated and expanded to include additional new resources, and includes a new section on gender and stereotyping. This book will be essential reading for anyone working with young women, including youth workers, PSHE teachers, pupil referral unit workers, Youth Offending Teams and voluntary sector youth leaders.